GOLF ARCHITECTURE
FOR NORMAL PEOPLE

ALSO BY GEOFF SHACKELFORD

The Riviera Country Club: A Definitive History

The Captain

Masters of the Links

The Good Doctor Returns

The Golden Age of Golf Design

Alister MacKenzie's Cypress Point Club

The Art of Golf Design

Grounds for Golf

The Future of Golf

Lines of Charm

Zenyatta At Home

GOLF ARCHITECTURE
FOR NORMAL PEOPLE

*Sharpening Your Course Design Eye
to Make Golf (Slightly) Less Maddening*

Geoff Shackelford

TATRA PRESS

Tatra Press LLC
Distributed by Independent Publishers Group, Baker & Taylor and Ingram
Cover design by Mimi Bark
Interior design by Isabella Piestrzynska (Umbrella Graphics)

Special sales and permissions: Chris Sulavik (Tatra Press) at tatrapress@gmail.com
or 646-644-6236

Front cover image: North Berwick Golf Club (North Berwick, Scotland) by Geoff
Shackelford.

Printed and bound in the United States by Sheridan Group (Chelsea, MI)
Tatra Press 4 Park Trail Croton-on-Hudson, NY 10520 www.tatrapress.com

TATRA PRESS

For Mom, who lovingly encouraged a boy's passion for golf architecture.
And for Dad, who took me to so many unforgettable courses.

CONTENTS

PREFACE. 1

INTRODUCTION 4

Chapter 1
ATTAINING EXPERTISE AND RETAINING NORMALCY
Understanding the perks and boundaries of course connoisseurship 10

Chapter 2
**WHAT IS A GOLF COURSE AND LESSONS
FROM THE MOST TIMELESS ONE OF ALL**
*Why early courses speak to what still matters…
and a few words about St Andrews* 17

**INTERMISSION: A SHORT GLOSSARY BEFORE
CRACKING THE CONNOISSEURSHIP CODE.** 34

Chapter 3
**R FOR REMEMBER: CAN YOU RECALL
SOMETHING ABOUT EACH HOLE?**
Course routing, variety of holes and sticky-but-surmountable features **41**

Chapter 4
**E FOR EVERY DAY: COULD YOU PLAY THE
COURSE EVERY DAY AND NEVER TIRE OF IT?**
Experience, playability and strategic intrigue **64**

Chapter 5
**D FOR DOG FRIENDLINESS: A COURSE
WHERE YOU'D TAKE A DOG FOR A WALK**
Scale, walkability, drainage and natural beauty **83**

Chapter 6
**TESTING R-E-D: CONFLICT AVOIDANCE,
THE RANKINGS, R-E-D NUMBERS,
MATCH PLAY(ING) AND BUCKET LISTING?**
Other fun ways to enjoy golf architecture without losing your mind **106**

Chapter 7
**EASY WAYS TO OUTSMART THE DESIGN: READING THE
ARCHITECT'S MIND AND SCORING BETTER**
Aerial recon, studying local knowledge and other ways to improve. **122**

APPENDIX—LISTS AND RESOURCES **149**

ACKNOWLEDGMENTS **161**

ABOUT THE AUTHOR. **163**

PREFACE

Beyond the fact that it is a limitless arena for the full play of human nature, there is no sure accounting for golf's fascination. Obviously yet mysteriously, it furnishes its devotees with an intense, many-sided, and abiding pleasure unlike that which any other form of recreation affords.

HERBERT WARREN WIND, golf writer

From every conceivable perspective, golf is preposterous.

The routines and rituals. The enormous scale of meticulously maintained landscapes for players to whap a ball with tungsten-infused tools. Plus the clothes. The yips. The swing. Arguments over nothing. Above all, the absurdity of "playing" something "fun" that's capable of crushing your dignity within minutes of your greatest feat. Why does golf even exist when every other ball-and-stick game that inspired the Scots expired long ago?

The golf courses.

A well-designed course on a beautiful day, played with even moderately tolerable company, becomes a place we'll remember long after the clubs have been locked in winter storage. Or for good. No other sport offers a comparable variety of settings and formats contested on what amounts to glorified obstacle courses that combine art, science, nature, storytelling, politics, business, agronomy and landscape architecture.

Yet for all the billions spent annually by weekenders just to play at the local muni, on up to the lucky few who travel the world for the next eye-opening golf experience, there has never been a straightforward guide to enjoying the finer design details. Or a road map to sniffing out the pretenders that course aficionados can spot in no time.

Voilà! *Golf Architecture for Normal People.*

I intend, to the best of my abilities as a longtime observer, writer, golf course architect, and retired competitive golfer, to help you:

- Derive more enjoyment from oddly hatched concoctions called "golf courses."
- Analyze a design so you can credibly explain what you love or loathe about a course and do so without causing irrevocable strife.
- Play better golf by knowing just enough to dissect the architecture proficiently, maybe to the point you can forget about the four swing triggers.
- Put bloviating course architecture geeks—guilty here as charged—in their place for waxing about Tillinghast's overuse of reverse-cambered double doglegs in his post-Shawnee years.
- Along the way, learn about how the sport evolved, all while experiencing dated references, analogies, metaphors, idioms and similes that might prompt some readers to ask questions such as: "Alexa, what is *Citizen Kane?*"

- Conclude without a reasonable doubt that golf courses need to welcome dogs more often.

For years, golf architecture was seen as too "inside baseball"—a snooty, dry and elusive topic exclusive to golf's cognoscenti who hold the best courses hostage. There are kernels of truth in that takeaway. But the enlightened 21st-century player is increasingly tapping into the simple pleasures of discovering, debating and dreaming about golf architecture. Never in two hundred and fifty or so years of documented golf history have so many golfers added "course design connoisseur" to their profiles or wanted to be better versed in the basics of constructive design criticism. Plenty more want to understand why some courses resonate, why some stink and, when necessary, how to justify their assessments to a 19th hole jury. That's why I'm so excited about this little scavenger hunt we're about to embark upon.

INTRODUCTION

GOLF n. & v. A game, probably evolved from Dutch antecedents, first recorded in Scotland in the 15ᵗʰ century, and played under codified rules since the middle of the 18ᵗʰ century; now consisting of hitting a golf ball, using an array of golf clubs, by successive strokes into each of nine or eighteen holes on a golf course.

PETER DAVIES, *Historical Dictionary of Golfing Terms*

What makes one golf course appealing enough to occasionally play different from another you'd sacrifice a limb to try just one time? Or feel like a spectacularly missed opportunity providing few reasons to ever return?

Why are some places a joy to play without having been declared a Best New Somewhat Affordable Signature Masterpiece? What makes a course feel special? And why do some courses just rub you the wrong way? Why, oh, why?

Such supposedly enigmatic questions have been debated since Scots began whapping beechwood spheres around grassy Edinburgh tracts, all while wagering and imbibing God-knows-what. Those early pioneers played through old artillery mounds, wore lots of scratchy tweed and smelled only slightly better than the nearby docks where many labored by day. But those avant-couriers were hooked. For at least a century, they risked legal and sectarian scorn to keep golfing.

So revelatory was this burgeoning offshoot of other ball-and-stick pastimes, that golf ventured out of the city and on to pastures considered unsuitable to farm but idyllic for bump-and-run shots. Since those wild and zany 1500s, golfers have debated the merits of one links course over another. Plenty more—okay, pretty much everyone who's taken a backswing — fancies him or herself as an armchair architect who could have done a little better. Don't fight the urge. This is a membership perk for all the agony and expense this silly sport inflicts.

Nearly five hundred years later—give or take lulls for wars and pandemics—we are still trying to settle the questions of golf's architectural charm and endurance. Perhaps more so now than at any point in history— thanks to the 75 million playing in the game worldwide, who realize how much the course and its tactical presentation factors into their passion for playing, watching and improving.

Not since the Jazz Age, when most of your First Team, All-World designs were created by brand names such as Donald Ross, Alister MacKenzie and A.W. Tillinghast, have golfers demanded more sophisticated designs and sensibly planned facilities for enjoyment during their precious leisure time. This architectural appreciation age has translated into robust comments sections, Tweets, reviews, rankings, podcasts, YouTube shorts and other forums to liven up post-round conjecture and life as a

A drone image of Cruden Bay's par-3 4th hole offers a perspective only previously available to birds or helicopter pilots. (Ru Macdonald)

golfer. The names of architects once barely known to golfers now appear on the front of scorecards. Drone imagery shows off courses from a hawk's perspective and increases our fascination with the art form. With online tools and satellite imagery, a golfer can scout out any course on the planet before going there and, as detailed in Chapter 7, save a few strokes by doing so. And unlike all other sports, we know there will always be more designs to conquer. Chew on that, pickleball!

Unbeknownst to most golfers, the mere act of picking up a club entitles you to course architecture connoisseurship. It's in your DNA, so don't resist. Yet the fundamentals necessary for refining a critical eye have traditionally been the stuff of rare books and intimidating online forums, which sometimes morph into mortal combat over perfunctory stuff.

Ground view of the same hole is not nearly as dramatic. (Geoff Shackelford)

As someone who has written about architecture and dabbled in it for over thirty years, I've observed an intensifying curiosity from golfers and welcomed their increased desire to know just enough to get more enjoyment out of the game. This book is for all golfers, including those well-intentioned souls who've made golf course design conjecture more complex than it needs to be. We might even tear down a few walls along the way. If ever a sport needed a little shaking up now and then, it's the royal and ancient game, often taken from its Scottish roots down some untenable paths by importers to new territories.

Many unfortunate design diversions were inspired by top players who believe their views reign supreme. And while good golfers can visualize and execute shots that lesser players cannot, most outstanding golfers are hardly like the artists you'd expect to see in Montmartre, brush in hand, sporting a beret and grappling with profound influences on the human condition.

The 13th green at Rustic Canyon. (Geoff Shackelford)

Here's the first big secret I'm going to reveal: Elite golfers tend to be selfish. They live off intoxicating whiffs of narcissism derived from pulling off shots that the rest of us can't envision, much less play. But this cockiness also makes them more likely to praise the difficulty or "test" in a course, effectively ignoring what charms 99 percent of the golf population. Subsequently, way too many courses are built or modified only to please this class of golfer with the loudest voice in the industry and the ear of those bankrolling new designs.

It should be noted that many of these elites became decent at golf by—how do I put this deftly—living free of excessive peripheral vision. Or, as Sir Walter Simpson said back in 1897, the "more fatuously vacant the mind is, the better for play." To which he added, "it has been observed that absolute idiots play the steadiest."

Walter's words, not mine.

Creating golf courses around the demands of better players often results in an overemphasis on quantifying the design and evaluation of courses at the expense of what draws us to the world's most interactive and, at its best, mysterious art form. The most enjoyable courses let us win now and then. Yet, throughout golf history, select killjoys have successfully imposed a perverse belief that great courses are directly tied to their scoring resistibility. These point missers fail to recognize how wildly unusual a golf course is on the spectrum of artistic creations. Nor do they grasp the complexity of natural forces to be managed just to get one built—especially one with supreme craftsmanship able to satisfy all skill levels.

Perhaps this is why the amazing interactivity of these artistic creations gets overlooked. Just think: You can't step into Monet's depiction of his garden in the Louvre, amble about and experience Giverny, and enjoy a glass of wine. But in golf you can. It's an experiential art form. You can plan a trip to some exotic course and study the history, evolution and rationale behind the design. Then, through the magic of guest hours or kind hosts, employ your fourteen paint brushes to experience an emotional and physical adventure. Your eyes are opened to new worlds every time you embark on these immersions. Course by course, you become a connoisseur. Best of all? It did not cost you $88 million to hang on your castle wall.

Nor can you watch *The Godfather*, enter the wedding scene and help yourself to some cake while coyly eavesdropping on Luca Brazi as he nervously mumbles outside the Don's office. But in golf? We have everything from blockbusters to indie art house flicks to accessible YouTube starter videos for golfers to enjoy as they see fit (or gain access to).

The conversation around what genuinely makes for a great course needs a reboot. It's time to take the focus of design analysis away from hard numbers, superficial excess and those who subscribe to a bloated-is-better mentality. That mentality has suckered one too many developers into catering to magazine-ranking criteria or delusional dreams of hosting a championship. Before we reach the easy-to-remember questions that can make course design analysis accessible and enriching, a few words about "expertise."

Chapter 1

ATTAINING EXPERTISE AND RETAINING NORMALCY

*Understanding the perks and boundaries
of course connoisseurship*

*Every golfer worthy of the name should have some acquaintance
with the principles of golf course design, not only for the betterment
of the game, but for his own selfish enjoyment.*

BOBBY JONES

This book will facilitate your course design analysis and teach you how to cut through the occasional pomposity of experts, but we should also remain cognizant of the role criticism and discourse play before resorting to excessive mocking. For all the amusement to be derived from tossing grass clippings up to test hot winds of nonsense blowing your way, next time when confronted with an authority (self-proclaimed or otherwise), listen carefully to what he or she declares to be "great" architecture. Or why a course fails. Some of it will be profound and educational. Most of it will have little to do with fun.

During various dark holes of golf history, golfers have not asked enough questions of the experts, deferring to a wide array of dullards, frustrated accountants and a few hucksters with elixirs to sell. This prompted the art of course design to veer down several dreary dead ends. But early 21st-century scrutiny of design has emerged for a host of reasons, including changing values, course-rating panelists calling BS to stupid judging categories and a generational shift. Increasingly when evaluating what really matters, vanity and excess are starting to finish behind engagement and gratification.

This democratization of golf course design connoisseurship has even begun to force some experts to reconsider what matters. I plead guilty (only occasionally) to ignoring what gives a course meaning and permanence for most golfers. But I'm not normal when it comes to looking at a golf course. I notice weird little details and can't let it go when I see lazy and expensive nonsense, particularly when the design could have been more sustainable without torturing all who step onto the first tee.

Full confession: I've been known to go full-Miles.

Fans of Alexander Payne's *Sideways* know about the intense lead character, played by the irascible Paul Giamatti. He's forever remembered as a lovable, wine-drinking windbag, able to bury his nose in a glass and, upon closing his eyes, pressing on his ear tragus to detect notes of strawberry, the faintest "soupçon of asparagus" and a "nutty Edam cheese."

To which Jack, his dufus horndog buddy, played delightfully by Thomas Haden Church, agrees. Up to a point.

"Strawberry, yeah, strawberries. Not the cheese."

The Mileses of the world can be such blowhards. But they also elevate winemaking precepts by holding producers to certain standards. This has a positive trickle-down effect all the way to the shelves of a gas station. But in the quest for perfection, arbiters of taste often lose sight of the big picture. While you might roll your eyes at an architecture critic who docks points for sloppy construction practices that deflect our nifty bump-and-run approaches, we need higher standards demanded for the overall betterment of golf. The Mileses might pontificate about the routing's lack of variety in par-3 directions played, or rail on about excessive stuff that robbed a course of playability and affordability. But those insights also advance the art. Architects and developers take notice. They even take some criticism to heart and make changes. But this book is not for Miles and his ilk, at least not all of them.

Rather, it's for the Jacks of golf who want to absorb just enough to refine sensibilities and better understand the difference between some courses, while identifying what elements made you love one layout a little bit more. Feel free to take a more intense interest in the details from there, and I'm confident you'll derive more pleasure from your golf. But I offer this surgeon-general-like warning now and throughout: As you mull what genuinely makes a course worth returning to, you could grow irrationally annoyed by the side effects of golf's bizarre infatuation with building courses that could host a U.S. Open. Or wonkier stuff, like a lazy cart path addition that discourages a drive down the right side since a tee ball could easily reach the concrete and bounce out of bounds, thus negating the entire point of the hole, ruining your day and maybe even your hope for humanity.

Nor is it the fault of design critics that golf equipment rules are the same for everyone. This has meant a select few who play in The Masters are part of every design discussion, often unfairly inspiring changes to courses not called Augusta National. The pros play a very different game with equipment custom fit to their extreme clubhead speed, now exacerbated in the 21st century by a generation who grew up learning to swing faster thanks to the lightest and sturdiest shafts ever made. In developing a sharper eye, you will notice this silly pursuit of the pro-game standards at the everyday level and might well get annoyed when you realize the sport now needs north of 7,500 yards for back tees to test a pro.

These revelations, and the satisfaction you'll derive, will only bring more gusto in those moments when nature, the architect and the superintendent creatively conspired to present an idyllic commingling of sensations. Throw in some late magic hour light and you might even think you've landed in Golf Heaven.

Which brings us back to obsessive Miles, who infamously threatened Jack outside a central California restaurant before an awkward double date.

"If anyone orders merlot, I'm leaving. I am NOT drinking any f$%#@&^ merlot!"

Post-*Sideways*, merlot sales declined by two percent over three years, while Miles's beloved pinot noir experienced an eight percent spike in sales and a production increase of roughly 170 percent. A funny movie line was taken seriously. Maybe excessively so.

While a more refined grape became more popular and piqued interest in nuanced wines to a larger audience, the rush to brand merlot as the golf course equivalent of a dirt polo field unfairly ridiculed the grape—one that happened to produce a satisfying, maintainable and affordable experience for plenty of oenophiles.

Not to over-press the wine metaphor, but golf is rife with plenty of above-average merlots that may not make any Top-100 lists. Those solid designs won't ever host a PGA Tour event or dazzle the golf-ranking panel-ists with the greatest "comfort stations" (a.k.a. free snack bars with free booze at rich-people places). But these courses also never get dull and may have more clever, understated characteristics than most care to take the time—or perhaps have the discernibility—to notice. They do not cost a ton to play and make plenty of people feel welcome playing a sport that's relentlessly uncomfortable. These merlots feature enough subtle touches and occasional heart-pumping thrills to keep you coming back. They may not offer the golf architectural equivalent of an Edam cheese and probably could be improved with some sound tweaks or improved maintenance to ensure graceful aging. But they also maybe fit the land, offer moments of drama and evoke an emotional attachment, even if your game isn't always able to overcome what the architect delivered.

That's why I believe three simple questions can help anyone—hard-core critic or new connoisseur of courses—to answer everything that sepa-rates the outstanding from the merely solid, to the total hot messes. These inquiries form the basis of similar questions asked by the most trusted critics I know, only in an easier fashion to remember.

Yes, against my better judgment, I'm offering a system.

The only acronym-based analytic approaches I endorse are those that win me money at the racetrack. However, kids, as you age, the mind matures, making an easy-to-remember system quite practical and far less compli-cated than the onslaught of criteria such as rules median scores and other nonsense that Top-100 panelists are forced to consider when evaluating a course. Since this is no Agatha Christie mystery and you've already seen the table of contents, here are the three monumentally simple questions we'll pose when evaluating a golf courses through fresh eyes and with plain old common sense.

(R)emember: Can you remember every hole? The ability to recall all or most of a course speaks to a bunch of vital stuff, from the variety and sequencing, to whether there were enough memorable details as you turned out the entrance drive and went on your merry way, replaying the round in your mind's eye. This question primarily addresses a beloved go-to topic of hard-core "architecturalistas": the routing. The hole sequencing can make or break a course in the same way an album or playlists can provide coherence to a collection of songs. But excessive and snooty routing analysis can also tip you off to golf architectural gas-baggery! We explore this and more in Chapter 3.

(E)very day: Is it a course you could play every day and never tire of? Most golfers know what layout they'd dream of playing if only allowed one in perpetuity. But the question, as posed here, speaks to what all but total masochists believe to be golf architecture's secret sauce: Is the course playable and filled with enough thought-provoking moments to keep the place compelling daily? And, in a painful concession to human nature, and its deep connection to that of our canine brethren, I will also concede another aspect of the Every Day question liable to make me the object of scorn by the intelligentsia. Details to come in Chapter 4.

(D)ogs: Is this a place you can take your dog for a walk? This topic may be interpreted two ways and I encourage both. Primarily, dog walkability first speaks to scale. If it's a place Fido or Toto love sniffing around, there is likely to be a natural flow, feel and calming effect to the course. The landscape is one that can be enjoyed without your golf clubs, as evidenced by the wildlife that are drawn to its quiet beauty. Artists see scenes for painting landscapes. And, secondly, actual dog friendliness says a lot about a facility. Some of the greatest clubs and courses in the world welcome our furry friends and have for centuries. Most don't. Maybe we'll change that in Chapter 5.

And there it is.

R-E-D

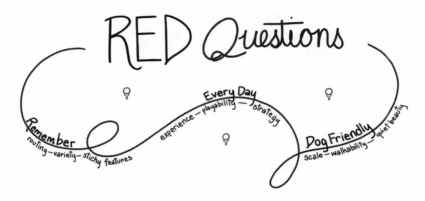

R-E-D diagram. (Illustrated by Nicole Prado)

Not my favorite color, by the way. It's been known to indicate danger or alarm. Or worse. I bleed Dodger blue and prefer when the Rams wear their blue uniform tops. My parents went to UCLA (light blue). I played golf in college at Pepperdine (navy blue). Nearly all the rivals to these epic institutions wear some shade of red.

Anyway, I digress. So now that we have my color allegiances on the record, let's set the table by understanding a bit more about how this silly sport started and why design fundamentals from several hundred years ago will immediately make you a keener design aficionado.

Chapter 2

WHAT IS A GOLF COURSE
AND LESSONS FROM
THE MOST TIMELESS ONE OF ALL

*Why early courses speak to what still matters...
and a few words about St Andrews*

Trying to find the origin of golf is as pointless as trying to discover who invented bread. Moreover, there is a danger that in making such research we might overlook the delights of both of them. There is another danger: if the work is done by an historian, he may bore the golfer with his erudite findings; if by a golfer he may be too ignorant of history to make a proper job of it.

PETER RYDE, writer

Books, lectures, papers and more books have tried to pin down the origins of golf. The most recent effort is devoted entirely to dispelling the liveliest tales regarding how the Dutch game of *kolf* morphed into Scotland's *gowf, golve, goff, goffing, gouf, gowff, golff* and finally, after consulting 16th-century brand-equity experts, golf.

There will forever be some uncertainty over whom deserves credit for what has become a vast international pastime of 38,000 courses with over 70 million humans identifying as golfers. The sport is now played in 206 of the world's 251 countries worldwide. The U.S. and its 16,000 courses account for 42 percent of the world's layouts, sustaining nearly two million jobs and an $84 billion industry.

From the beginning, one constant has persisted: Players start at a point, whap the ball around for several hours and (usually) finish near the starting point. But how golf ended up with the "course" and the notion of a golf architect have filled far fewer pages than stories of Mary Queen of Scots turning up at this or that place (which is about every course in Scotland, and she probably never played any of them). The ethereal happenstance of golf's birth and who ultimately legitimized the sport has proven to be a far more enticing subject of inquiry for historians than the history of early course design. You can't blame them. Golf's origin story mixes religion, royalty, rabbits and rogues. It was a tweedier and far less bloody "Game of Thrones" with dramatic shades of *A Midsummer Night's Dream* and "Downton Abbey" thrown into the mix.

Perhaps the murkiness surrounding golf architecture's beginnings is simply a product of the odd ways early courses evolved. But there are clues suggesting Scots were drawn to linksland on fallow seaside dunes with rabbit-maintained turfgrasses. Like ancient recipes, those formative years of golf course design were passed down by word of mouth and left

Leith Links circa 1827. (artist unknown)

undocumented in part because early golf was technically an illegal pursuit of the plebeian class.

Boy, did they flip that script!

The original golfers were winging it without the foggiest notion that their casually invented recreation would survive intact for centuries. They were probably having too much fun to document rules, golf course "design" or conventions as they evolved. It was a chance to get out in the fresh air and escape everyday doldrums. They were competing and building camaraderie that had nothing to do with livelihoods or trades. Plus, the golf was unfettered by boundaries. There were no rights, wrongs, magazine awards or liability laws imposing limitations. As for recording the first drafts of the game's history? For whatever reason, they took a mulligan.

For the purpose of honing in on what really matters, we can target the intangible qualities that clicked in early Scottish golf to unlock questions about why a vast majority of golfers are drawn to certain sensibilities and offended by others. Understanding what drew people to golf five-or-so centuries ago will unlock gut instincts and more astute observations. And you might even hate blind shots a little less.

> *In the sixteenth century, just as now, the long evenings of North Britain gave the workingmen three or four hours of good play after the day's labor was done. Scotsmen devoted their evenings so thoroughly to golf to the exclusion of archery that the Scottish Parliament, concerned at the greater proficiency of their English enemies with bow and arrow, decreed in 1457 that "ye football and ye golf be utterly cryt doune,' and provided for the setting up of archery butts for popular amusement. Obviously golf must have been played for many years to become a popular menace.*
>
> C.B. MACDONALD, golf architect

Ball and stick sports have been around for a few thousand years. According to Homer and backed up by Herodotus, those wild and zany Lydians on the Greek Isle of Corcyra were the first to use a ball designed for an outdoor pursuit. Specifically, a Spartan princess Anagalla deserves the credit. Who is going to quibble with Homer or Herodotus?

Fast-forward a few years to Rome and Julius Caesar, who took his mind off more pressing matters by playing *paganica* with feather-stuff leather balls, bent sticks and natural targets such as trees or boulders to play at. Depictions make *paganica* look a little like golf in togas.

Germans played something similar called *kolbe*. The French had their *jeu de mail* and the Dutch partook in a wintery sport called *kolf*

The Kolf Player by Rembrandt Harmensz van Rijn,1654. (Museum of Fine Arts, Boston)

with similarities to the German game, ice hockey and hints of curling for good measure. Most golf historians lean toward the Dutch as the key initiators of golf for pretty darn good reasons. But plenty of others aren't so sure and they generally have a funny way of pronouncing town as *toon*. These contrarians will even dismiss the Dutch as the key to golf by suggesting their renowned painters just did a better job of documenting history than other civilizations. Rembrandt sketched something with golf leanings to bolster that theory.

Still, most observers confidently say the Scots came up with golf from *kolf* since solid documentation exists of Dutch ships dropping anchor in the Edinburgh ports near Leith. They understandably brought their long

Leith Links today is a park with this plaque denoting the place where organized golf began. (Geoff Shackelford)

wooden sticks along to keep their games sharp, setting up shop on a large, open grassy area interrupted by hillocks, paths, ancient burial grounds and old military embankments. The Scots seemed to have joined in during the 16th century. Today, the same parcel is a flattened-out park. Golf started to move on to better playgrounds in the 1850s and was officially outlawed at Leith in 1905.

As crude as it might have seemed compared to later links, Leith's five holes ranged from 414 to 495 yards and offered firm, fescue grass grounds dotted by salty characters, occasional skirmishes over unpaid debts, and groups playing through picnicking families. At some point, a similar green space in St Andrews and other Scottish coastal ports popular for horseback riding saw these grassy grounds turn entirely to golf.

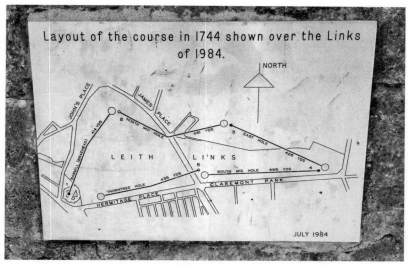

The original sequence of the five holes at Leith Links. (Geoff Shackelford)

So, regardless of what anyone else might claim, the Scots get credit for hitting a small, ball-adjacent rounds of beechwood or feather-stuffed leather around Leith and soon, another hillier spot in the city at a place near the Edinburgh Castle called Bruntsfield. They adopted basics of *kolf* to these strangely unlevel grounds once inhabited by the sea and where the ball was prone to bounce randomly off wave-like contours that no bulldozer has since been able to replicate. Unlike other ball and stick pursuits, this one had the addition of grass under foot and a more freewheeling sensibility, with fewer boundaries or known written clauses until 1744. That's when a Jacobite surgeon named Dr. John Rattray put ink to parchment and, in essence, the Honourable Company of Edinburgh Golfers became the originators of what we now call the Rules of Golf, governed today by the Royal and Ancient Golf Club of St Andrews and the United States Golf Association.

Of note, the alluring brevity and elegance of the original guidelines is downright dreamy compared to modern Rules of Golf and made even more amazing since around half of those original rules have no purpose today. But one guideline became a focal point: Play the ball as it lies and don't even think about touching, manipulating or mashing the ground surrounding your ball until you hole out. Or words to that effect.

Play it as it lies instilled that golf was an adventure of hitting the ball, finding it and hitting again until holing out. Early golf merged hunting and gathering, athletic freedom of expression and a test of character.

Hard by, in the fields called the Links, the citizens of Edinburgh divert themselves at a game called Golf. Of this diversion the Scots are so fond, that, when the weather will permit, you may see a multitude of all ranks, from the senator of justice to the lowest tradesman, mingled together, in their shirts, and following the balls with the utmost eagerness.

TOBIAS SMOLLETT, 1771, *The Expedition of Humphrey Clinker*

The Scots played the ball where they found it, even if this meant occasionally playing off a dirt path, cobblestone street, railroad track or out of Aunt Olivia's thistle garden overlooking the links. Unlike the Dutch game or croquet that came along in the 1850s, the golf ball had to be struck crisply and, occasionally, pitched airborne since there was no ice to send it across. The Scots took what was essentially long distance putting and added new dimensions suited to their linksland. A wider array of shots necessitated smaller, more specialized versions of the unwieldy Dutch implements. And thus was born the golf manufacturing industrial complex!

Even better, golfers could take liberties in what route they chose to

Early golf characters came in all shapes, sizes and expressions.

the hole instead of merely standing in the same location and seeing who hit the best shot from designated points. This freedom, when combined with the unpredictable leather-wrapped spheres stuffed tightly with feathers, personalized the playing of early golf. But lacking today's aerodynamically engineered dimple designs rigorously tested for maximum efficiency, "featheries" flew low and unpredictably. When they got wet, "featheries" fell apart. So, between the "flukiness," coarse ground and rough characters drawn to the occasional wager, golf was hardly a peaceful or easy outdoor jaunt. And Edinburgh isn't exactly Boca.

"One of the vilest climates under Heaven," wrote Robert Louis Stevenson. And he was a big fan of the place!

Yet for all the issues, they persisted in setting out on these hunts despite the obstacles.

The mid-19th-century introduction of gutta-percha golf ball manufacturing continued the momentum by lowering costs and allowing for more

1800s depiction of golf at Bruntsfield with the Edinburgh castle in the distance. (Bruntsfield Links Golfing Society)

reliable shotmaking. As the Scots kept refining clubs, balls and courses, the game spread to other linksland where, unlike other sports with designated grounds and lines, no two of these playgrounds were the same. Instead of letting this inconvenience hold them back, they recognized this variety as an asset. The linkslands next to town became a place to be. People were having fun watching or playing golf. They were getting fresh air and exercise. The happenstance and oddities added to the charm.

While plenty give royals excessive credit for validating golf as a burgeoning national pastime in the wild and crazy 1700s, this has never explained what drove people to play during those few hundred years of golf before the landed gentry made it cool by hopping in their horse-drawn

The Bruntsfield links today serves as both a pitch-and-putt and city center park where the castle remains visible. (Geoff Shackelford)

carriages and heading down from Holyrood Palace to play Leith or Bruntsfield. At least one of the seven King Jameses during this period publicly supported the game. While very nice of him, accounts of his support never explain why golf was first mentioned (and outlawed) in 1471, or how it carried on for a couple of centuries as an underground pursuit of soldiers, sportsmen and women, along with early sandbaggers who were supposed to be practicing their archery. Plenty of everyday citizens risked a 40-shilling fine or more if caught playing on Sunday. That offense came with forced repentance appearances at the following Sunday's services.

All this intrigue occurred in the city while Lord Grantham and friends were off hunting fox or shooting beautiful creatures out of the sky.

The upstairs crowd initially looked down upon what seemed like a rather pedestrian alternative to more refined (and typically inland) pursuits in the glorious countryside. Golf, however, offered a new way to indulge in the universal joy of competitive sport over Nature's rolling, expansive marvels. With no major confining elements, the strategy of figuring out how to get in the hole in fewer strokes (or, in a sense, sooner) than your opponent preserved the best of other sports. The kookiness of the conditions—whether they be tempestuous weather, bumps, burns, dunes or high sea grasses—necessitated strategic planning, also elemental in other sports.

While golf lacked jousting or other physical military skill, it made up handsomely in its cunning tactics of warfare needed to circumvent two forms of trouble: what the ball did when hitting the ground and how this affected a match against a human opponent. Most of all, there were (and remain) incontrovertible thrills in taking on a natural obstacle—a swale, mound or sandy hole left behind by Mother Nature—which, every once in a while, allowed the golfer to claim victory.

Whatever resemblances there are between golf and other ancient games, the simple truth remains that it was the Scots who first combined in a game the characteristics of hitting a ball cross country, to a hole in the ground without interference by an opponent.

CHARLES PRICE, golf writer

Early golf's cross-country sensibility that Price refers to might be hard for 21st-century golfers to imagine through a modern perspective of pre-ordained holes masterminded by blueprint-wielding golf course architects. With our more manicured courses and clearly delineated paths to the hole, cross-country play is only a thing of late evening shenanigans when

Wind did not discourage the Scots from pursuing gutta percha balls, as seen in this scene from North Berwick.

the pro shop staff has clocked out. But even with guideposts like trees, framing bunkers, homes lining the fairways and signs telling us where to go, modern golf still offers an incomparable journey.

The most engaging golf courses lure us in, feature plot twists and rarely seem desperate to make a first impression. This may explain why the obvious, straightforward design quickly grows stale while the ones with some bit of mystery endure. More importantly, the very best let us win. They do not *seem* manufactured even when they are.

For two hundred years or so, golf architecture has been in a constant tug-of-war between those who love the uber-natural and those who want to penalize every missed shot (usually golf pros hired to design a course who end up selfishly making something only they can handle). It's the difference between natural and artificial. Of restrained over forced. And free over constrained. This core principle is at the heart and soul of St Andrews, where a most soulful version of golf was experienced as the less romantic Leith faded away.

What would later become known as the "Old Course at St Andrews" confirmed to the Scots that they'd stumbled onto something far more magical than *kolf* or the early adaptations in Edinburgh. And yes, having one of the seven Jameses approving golf was a nice thing for the sport. But the lessons taught by this magical place in Fife drove golf to new places of magnificence.

From left-to-right, early golf visionaries and clubmakers: James Wilson, Willie Dunn, Bob Andrew, Willie Park, Tom Morris, Allan Robertson, Dawe Anderson, Bob Kirk.

The more I studied the Old Course, the more I loved it and the more I loved it, the more I studied it.

BOBBY JONES

No book about golf architecture would be complete without at least a dollop of appreciation for the Old Course. And you likely fall into one of three camps whenever this sacred spot is mentioned.

Camp one: *Really? Been there, done that. Looks weird to me.*

Camp two: *I don't get the fuss or know much about it, but maybe you'll enlighten me. Keep it brief.*

Camp three: *Wax, brother, wax! Say more about this magical place that transformed a crude game and can still test the best in golf centuries later.*

Even its greatest admirers will concede that golf over the Old Course

A postcard with Old Tom Morris preparing to tee off at St Andrews.

is not always a love-at-first-sight encounter. Its mysterious and cruel bounces have tended to bring out the comedic side of people you never knew could crack a joke.

Pro golfer Ed Furgol thought it needed a "dry clean and a press." Sam Snead said it looked like the "kind of real estate you couldn't give away" after eventually falling for its many charms. And despite massive changes in the equipment and maintenance over the centuries, the Old remains the most complex and endlessly unpredictable piece of golf architecture on the planet. It's the one course Bobby Jones, Jack Nicklaus and Tiger Woods have all admired most, declaring that it's where they'd play if only given one last round. The Old remains sacred ground to golf architecture's greatest minds, making it slightly embarrassing that no course designer has come close to matching its depth, originality, complexity and enchanting idiosyncrasies.

The global 18-hole standard is the product of St Andrews. But that's just a number. The Old Course gave birth to the idea of golf architecture as an art that could further our lives. The course evolved from a narrow corridor through gorse and into golf's grandest chess board created by nature, with vital early assists from characters named Allan Robertson, Old Tom Morris and the Strath family of golfers. As long as Scots have documented the sport, the Old Course provoked discussion and debate that no other links elicited. In doing so, the Old Course made the early pioneers cognizant of the links' role in a burgeoning sport.

Old Tom Morris, as photographed outside his shop by golf architect A.W. Tillinghast.
(Ralph W. Miller Golf Library)

Fifth hole on the Old Course at St Andrews. (Geoff Shackelford)

The Old survived vicious, almost fatal uproars, over rabbits and roads. In the lively pubs just steps from the course, the citizens of St Andrews debated design elements and the magical things taking place over the wild contours. They wondered how so many bunkers could so magically intervene in all the perfect places. And thanks to the historic university town's ancient churches and love of history, a supportive ecosystem nurtured golf's Sistine Chapel.

By serving as golf's North Star for centuries, the Old Course still compels visitors and regulars to wonder why it ages so well when other layouts tear at the seams. The Old opened eyes to the possibility that golf courses were works of art. It solidified golf's shift from a game board with ties to *kolf,* into a vast sporting field with artistic underpinnings and strategic cross-country qualities as the driving force in expanding golf to faraway places.

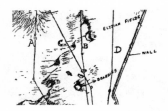

INTERMISSION: A SHORT GLOSSARY BEFORE CRACKING THE CONNOISSEURSHIP CODE

Golf's lexicon of colorful words and phrases is its crowning achievement. For long after the urge of the ability to play the game leaves us, golf's joyful adjective sand modifiers, its splendid superlatives and unequalled accolades ring in my ear the waves of a familiar sound.

ROBERT BROWNING, golf rules expert and writer

N ow that we've warmed up with a small bucket, it's almost time to settle golf architecture's biggest questions. But first, and with a full apology to Peter Davies's magnificent *Historical Dictionary of Golfing Terms*, a main source of, and inspiration for, definitions noted below, this is an opportunity to highlight vital definitions sometimes rudely hijacked by purists. Tuck them in your back pocket for safekeeping the next time you are sitting next to a member of the Golf Linguistics Police.

Course. Typically defined as 18 holes where the sport of golf is played. Handy fact if you ever get to play Golf Jeopardy: "Course" first appeared in 1823's *Delineations of St Andrews*, not the original rules of golf. Only recently has golf realized how a total of 18 holes—a direct link to St Andrews—is not always the best number for every site. The early courses prioritized what the land gave them. So whatever number they finished on proved adequate to the early pioneers not caught up in formulas. (For example, Leith was 5 holes, Prestwick 12.) In the 21st century, many courses were viewed as faux golf for failing to reach 18 and a par of 70 or higher. These would be your par-3, executive 9-holers. They are now considered essential to the future of the game and can be more attractive—and fun—alternatives to some "real" conventional courses.

Links. Rough, slightly hilly land shaped by the sea around two-hundred million years ago and later covered with a layer of sand after the last Ice Age meltdown. Found mostly in the United Kingdom, true links-land possesses indigenous soil type and plant life not found elsewhere. Some one hundred and fifty courses technically qualify as pure links. The definition of links has, over time, been expanded to describe any course near water where the weather is windy, the site treeless or some combination of both. Most of these are not true links. But in the interest of Normalcy, do not be the person to point this out. Just call them links-style and that'll shush the purists. The word "links" dates to 1623, when Sir R. Gordon wrote of Dornoch in totally spell-check-unfriendly dialect: "Along the sea coast ther ar the fairest and largest linkes (or green feilds) or any pairt of Scotland, fitt for archery, goffing, ryding and all other exercise."

Green. The maintained putting surface area where the hole is cut and tended to by a greenkeeper and hard-working staff. After you paid a green fee. The tendency to add an unnecessary "s" after green, while not a big deal, is also a telltale sign of a non-golfer for reasons not of material import to our greater golf architecture mission. Green once described the entire course because the areas for play were green spaces near towns. That's how the word originally emerged in printed record—in 1743's first poem devoted to *The Goff.* Since then, few others besides Judge Smails have called it *goff.* Also, to be noted when you get angry about a green that is too slow, fast, bumpy, tiered or neglected, remember that putting areas were initially not treated differently than other course areas for centuries. We have it good.

Hole. Most commonly describes the four-and-a-quarter-inch wide and (at least) four-inches deep cylinder-shaped excavation of the green where the ball must fall into for a score to be recorded as finished. Less common (yet still very prevalent throughout this book), is the relentless invocation of "hole" to describe the combination of tee, fairway, hazards and putting surface where we play golf. Useless fact: The first and most obvious use of hole could be found in 1744's rules by John Rattray. But a year earlier in *The Goff,* Thomas Mathison invoked "holes" in describing someone's rough start to a match.

Hole location. Refers to the placement of a cup (and flag inserted into it). In the ensuing chapters I will also use "pin placement" to reveal I'm a product of the 70s. Bowling was in then, and the inimitable Tommy Bolt first made "pin" a groovy word to use. ("The pin placements are grotesque," raged Mr. Bolt.) Pin positions works too. The word pin was first used by a golf poet in 1893, but most golf courses did not move the hole/cup/pin around daily until many decades later, negating the need for "location." Yet using "flagstick location" is a non-starter. The sport has reluctantly settled on the least painful option with hole location. To delineate today's spot where the journey comes to an end and the ball disappears into the subterranean, hole location works best. But if anyone tries to correct you on the use of pin, tell them it was good enough for P.G. Wodehouse over a hundred years ago.

Tee. The area where play begins on a hole. Tee is a derivative of the Scottish *teaz* with some Latin thrown in to imply "support." Early on, golfers used sand to prop up a ball from the starting area of each hole. When players tired of sandy messes left behind, wooden pegs were invented in the early 20th century, and a dual meaning originated. The words "teeing ground" and "tee box" also work for the starting point of a hole. Beware: Some find adding "box" as a suffix offensive even when many tees are shaped like boxes.

Dogleg. Term to describe non-linear golf holes and widely used in society to describe anything with a bend. Some of the best and most pronounced "doglegs" would not function on a canine, but they sure make great holes (see the 13th at Augusta National.) Any par-3 labeled a dogleg is about the worst compliment you can pay. Unless it's the 16th at Cypress Point or some other option-laden long one in a beautiful locale. As much as our golfing predecessors loved dogs, they were not initially keen on holes with a defined bend. In the August, 1902, U.K. version of *Golf Illustrated*, the first dogleg-adjacent reference appeared in print. "This hole," they wrote in 1902, "has been criticized by some

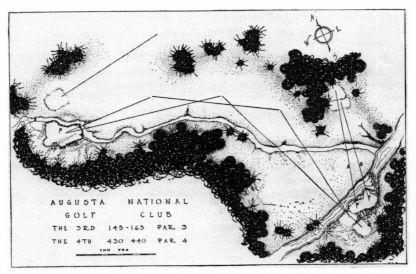

The most famous "dogleg" hole in golf as rendered at the time with help from architect Alister MacKenzie. (1932 *Golfers Yearbook*)

on the ground that the player cannot play straight for the hole, the line for which is rather like a dog's hind leg." Zing!

Bunker. A concave depression in the ground covered with sand. These "hazards" come in varying sizes, depths and presentation styles often over-maintained at extravagant expense to prevent temper tantrums from otherwise well-mannered adults. "Sand trap" is not preferable. But even the best-educated and most eloquent golfer of all time, Bobby Jones, used "trap" on occasion. Unlike those who take personal umbrage by the use of sand trap, I will not judge. Just go with bunker to avoid needless admonition from people sporting multiple course logos from exclusives places where they are not a member. Bunker,

Bunkers come in all sizes and styles. (Geoff Shackelford)

it should also be noted, is a St Andrews special and first appeared in 1812's *Regulations for the Game of Golf*. Leith and Bruntsfield did not have bunkers, just embankments, swales, dirt patches and pickpockets.

Hazard. Any architectural feature that inflicts misery and added strokes to your score. Bunkers, gorse, creeks, lakes, ponds, ditches, barrancas, canyons, swamps, marshes, bays and oceans are just some of the more common hazards referenced going forward. How these are incorporated into a design can make the difference between fun and misery, intrigue and dread, or a naturally seductive course and a forcibly manufactured mess. Hazard was first used in the original code by Rattray and has been central to the golf lexicon until, in 2019, it was excised from the official Rules of Golf in favor of the loathsome "penalty area." It's a crime. "Dottie, could you tell if his ball crossed the line?" asks the lead announcer. "Yes, Jim, he's found the haz…the penalty area."

Local knowledge. A widely used phrase almost surely traceable to golf, this one first made a printed page in the August 8, 1887, issue of the *Glasgow Herald*. That's where they indirectly mentioned the importance of an "intimate acquaintance with the green has enabled a local player to carry off with the coveted medal." Horace Hutchinson used the phrase after the century turned and Bobby Jones even suggested golfers rely too much on local knowledge in judging distances. My how times have changed, with golfers relying on technological tools for guidance while neglecting the art of accumulating place-based insights. (Local knowledge is just one more asset making golf courses different than all other sports venues and is explored to save you strokes in Chapter 7.)

Golf architecture. Initially labeled "Green Architecture" in the late 1800s by John Anderson, secretary of Mortonhall Golf Club. Subsequently, architect Herbert Fowler invoked "links architecture" in 1907. The architectural duo of Colt & Alison published *Some Essays On Golf Architecture* in 1920 and George Thomas tightened things up with 1927's *Golf Architecture in America*. The phrase describes the theory, practice, vision, design and occasional ingeniousness of the golf courses we play.

Chapter 3

R FOR REMEMBER:
CAN YOU RECALL SOMETHING
ABOUT EACH HOLE?

*Course routing, variety of holes
and sticky-but-surmountable features*

*When you play a course and remember each hole, it has individuality
and change. If your mind cannot recall the exact sequence of the holes,
that course lacks the great assets of originality and diversity.*

GEORGE THOMAS, golf architect

The clubs have been lovingly placed into the car trunk and you're headed back down Magnolia-ish Lane. This is when wise, determined golfers will start counting how many greens in regulation they hit. Or, after particularly grim days, drawing up the six most dramatic ways to quit the game. (Based on Instagram posts, hurling all fourteen clubs into a pond is the most satisfying and least grow-the-game friendly option. Donate people, donate.) More emotionally stable golfers will see this post-round commute as a chance to get better. Keep stats if such number crunching floats your boat. Draw the line at Strokes Gained. That's a cry for help.

What could have been better?

Why did I rush the shot on 14?

Do I really want to play another round with that cheating donkey?

At least I didn't die today trying to scale Mount Everest.

Architecture nuts use this drive time to consider the layout just played or get into a spirited design debate with carpoolers. Leaving the course also provides the ideal time to play armchair architect or, if carpooling, play a match between the holes from a layout down the street (more on that fun process comes in Chapter 6). Not until I got a little older and more absent-minded did the memorability factor become a strong indicator of more than my cerebral cortex's health. If we can't distinguish a set of 18 holes just minutes removed from playing them, this might be a pretty good indicator something about the design is amiss.

The "Remember" test came into focus many years ago after playing a newly constructed private course on a glorious property. A magazine commissioned me to gush over the deep, hidden genius within its insipid 18 holes. While heading down an entrance drive carved at great expense, I began working through the holes to imagine how I'd turn this boiled hot dog into a prime tenderloin. The publication in question was cajoled into enlisting me to slobber over its visionary creators, all so they could frame the article on their office wall. So no matter what brilliant constructive criticism

I might slip into the story, the editor would chop it out to avoid blowback from the course.

While keeping both eyes on the road, my hole-by-hole sorting process began. Were there any standouts I could write about as world beaters? Let's see.

The first two? No problem. It's rare to forget the openers. You're nervous on the first tee and any feature—from OB to a simple fairway bunker—usually sticks. Plus, you probably just walked by the first tee again. After the openers? I struggled to recall any concrete detail about the third hole before recalling its par and that it was surrounded by tall trees. And, breaking news, the fourth did have a lake on the right!

Memories, light the corners of my mind!

In this case, the architect sorta, kinda provided incentive to drive down one side of the fourth fairway—mostly to avoid the water—while *maybe* shortening the hole ten yards. Not exactly robust layers of Machiavellian strategy, but it was a start.

This aggressively billed high-end masterpiece became a blur for the next dozen or so holes. There were a few *misty water-colored* memories of the general hole directions and dogleg shapes. The pars were, at best, *scattered pictures* in my mind. I could at least recall how the 9th and 10th played uphill to the clubhouse and delivered me near a far more memorable (grilled) hot dog with a delicately toasted brioche bun. The brain fog thickened until my much younger, sharper mind easily recalled the two finishing holes. And only because (A) I had just played them thirty minutes before, and (B) the holes did so very little to cap off the round in style.

The day confirmed how memorability highlights what we love about some courses compared to those we never need to play again. Little about the sequence of holes, the change of direction, noteworthy bunker placement, green contouring or how a beautiful backdrop was incorporated and stood out mere moments after playing. Just to be sure, I started going through the holes of a classic course played two days prior. I could easily piece together all 18, along with the key design touches that would make my next round there even more intriguing.

At that stage of my golf architecture education, I was trained to believe that the recall factor was a rather shallow criterion for greatness—or even a dangerous one. This was the 1990s, when new courses were designed more as a subject for golf-course photography than for playability. Many were built to appease strange forces searching for the longest, prettiest, fairest and most difficult "tests" of golf. A counter-minimalist movement was in the early stages of resetting values and believed the celebration of "memorable" holes would only lead to silly special effects, thus making courses more expensive to build and even less fun to play. This was also peak Pete Dye.

Golf is not a fair game, so why build a course fair?

PETE DYE

The most prominent, successful and charmingly insane designer of the day was regularly loathed for his eccentrically excessive designs. Nothing made him happier than to hear golfers gripe! But he could also be formulaic. Pete loved double dogleg par-5s snaking through two lakes and calling on two distinct shot shapes to shorten the hole. Or he loved finishing with a par-3 at the 17th surrounded by lots of trouble, then followed by a dogleg left long par-4 with water. He even routed the TPC Sawgrass on the back of a napkin now displayed in the clubhouse. (It was a flat property loaded with enormous snakes, so maybe he wasn't wrong to minimize romps through the swamp in search of cool native features.)

Pete Dye's 11th at TPC Sawgrass, one of many examples of a double dogleg par-5 calling for one shot shape off the tee and another for the next shot. (Geoff Shackelford)

For all the formulas and bombast Dye brought to his work, I never struggled to remember each of the holes right after leaving. Or months later. Sometimes when he put thirty pot bunkers on a hole and a bazillion railroad ties everywhere, the finer details became a blur in his entertainingly sadistic manner. But rarely did he build forgettable holes that only moved you from one location to another.

My design hero, the great amateur architect George Thomas, was quoted at the start of this chapter preaching memorability. He nailed it way back in 1927: When you can't recall the order of the holes or some of the differentiating qualities gifted by Mother Nature, such fogginess generally exposes a flawed or weak design. Consequently, the first acid test of any design can be answered by a simple question that speaks to several complex design questions: Can you Remember every hole soon after playing the course?

This will unlock three key design insights:

- The routing, a.k.a. the sequence of holes.
- The variety of pars, changes of direction or bends to the holes.
- Sticky but surmountable features—those concrete design touches that lodge in your brain without causing three-group backups on every tee.

ROUTING

> *It is impossible in considering types of holes for a course to suggest any positive sequence of alignment, for each layout should be designed to fit the particular ground on which it lies...*
>
> WILLIAM FLYNN, golf architect

Other than the topography, soil quality, budget and the mental well-being of the developer, there is no more vital component to a successful project than the way hole sequencing is determined. The routing. Or in certain non-Scottish circles where it's pronounced "rooting." Plenty of courses have been set down on land without regard for the people who will have to play there. So you would not be out of line to wonder if the architect angrily sketched out the sequence during a root canal.

"Routing" is occasionally hijacked to strongly suggest that the designer had divined some abstruse philosophical meaning, impenetrable to more pedestrian thinkers. It's unclear just how or when the word "routing" ever snuck into the golf lexicon—a rogue linguistic stowaway, of sorts. Nowhere in the history of golf has routing even been an identifiable word and it did not make the thorough *Historical Dictionary of Golfing Terms*. But, oh, how it's a fantastic way to spot a gasbag supreme.

"I didn't really care for the routing," you'll hear. Or "Richard Bobby Crook III really didn't route this very well." Or "There were not enough reverse cambers in his par-4s" is another golf equivalent of describing a wine as "oaky."

We as golfers have been known to gripe about redundancies in the sequence of holes or lack of originality when the course has too many dogleg right par-4s (when we consistently hit a distinctive righthander's draw.) But these are more issues of variety and creativity than they are of placement. It's a stretch to fervently declare that a routing is flawed unless you saw the blank canvas and watched the process evolve during meetings with the owners, agencies, bankers or land planners. There is little chance you could know what a rat's nest of obstacles and compromises the architect had to make, unless he shared every conceivable thought in an online discussion forum.

We won't know, for example, if the golf architect had to incorporate, say, the loan officer's affinity for courses that close with a long par-4. Or if the person signing the checks drove the land plan, oblivious to golf while prioritizing real estate sales. Or it could be something personal. Maybe the developer has a wicked slice and rejected a nice first hole where a boundary would have been in play to the right, setting him up for certain failure at the outset of his round.

A multi-volume set could be filled with stories of routings changed to deal with environmentally sensitive areas and other non-golf matters. Some of the routing tug-of-war tales are fascinating. Occasionally you even find out the course design improved when a new line of thinking was forced on the architect. But most of the stories of altered routings range from tedious to infuriating. Or somewhere in between.

Samuel Morse, the visionary behind the Pebble Beach development, told architect Alister MacKenzie that he would not get the desired oceanfront

Cypress Point long before golf holes. (Pacific Novelty Co.)

land at a new private course to be built in the late 1920s. MacKenzie had a special 14th hole in the works. But Morse had already gifted MacKenzie and co-architect Robert Hunter land for the 15th, 16th and 17th holes on one of the most beautiful meetings of land and sea. Early century postcards of this spot, called Cypress Point, featured covered wagons returning from taking in the stunning view, long before Morse allowed Marion Hollins to develop the famous 16th and 17th holes there.

But Morse was building a tourist destination. The centerpiece would continue to be the 17-Mile Drive, already in place as a dirt road. He intended to keep the drive special at a time automobiles were becoming commonplace. So Morse the visionary held firm and preserved the coastline view instead of letting it be exclusive to country club members. Nonetheless, the architects pushed back. Letters were written. Pleas made. In a plot twist everyone saw coming, the guy signing the checks won. And it all worked

The 14th tee at Cypress Point today. The architects wanted to bring the ocean more into play but developer Samuel Morse prioritized the 17th Mile Drive. (Geoff Shackelford)

out fine for a course that most people would give a limb to play. Yes, a par-4 14th would have been spectacular hugging the coastline. But it all worked out despite this concession to tourism. And even the most astute architecture critic is unlikely to know this went on unless they read my book on the place. So no one really wonders why the 14th plays where it does thanks to the way the 17-Mile Drive fits in and the magnitude of that famous road.

Routing analysis can turn aggravating when you learn the course was created off-site by otherwise able-bodied adults staying in their offices and relying on topographic maps and plotting functional needs over form—especially when they should have been walking the ground to soak up details that a golfer would appreciate. Features such as surprise vistas, potentially beautiful natural hazards, specimen trees hidden by junky shrubs or even simple little swales worth preserving. Planning out the order and placement of holes is also a wildly subjective art and one at the mercy of multiple possible whims: the architect's marching orders, how far the ball flies, drainage issues and environmental complications. Routing can be a frustrating game of finding the least-awful compromise.

I'm certain that the three greatest to ever play the game came to their conclusions about the need to regulate distance after working in golf architecture. Bobby Jones, Jack Nicklaus and Tiger Woods have all been in favor of distance regulation. And never out of an attempt to hoard more trophies to themselves. They all worked on design projects and undoubtedly ran out of space as more advanced weaponry allowed players of their day to strike the ball farther. Nothing pains a designer like finding land and features for a perfect do-or-die par-5 that must become something else due to a lack of space. All three legends have spoken out against the crushing cost increases prompted by a need for more acreage when the course footprint is constantly expanding.

As an architect, it's risky to recap these tales of routing woe without causing heads to bob like bored bobbleheads. Even when concessions lead to finding a hidden puzzle piece or fresh hole idea, routing talk is tedious stuff to all but the hardcore geekery. But forgive them if they start waxing on. Routing a course can also be the quietest, most fascinating time in an architect's life, so bear with them if they start waxing on about those special times walking the virgin land and finding holes. They were channeling that inner child who sketched dream holes on paper or geekily shaped them in beach sand while the cool kids surfed.

But for Normal People focused on settling big questions, there is little use in learning too much about the routing process if you hope to enjoy golf course connoisseurship. Like watching a film where you remain oblivious to script revisions, extra scenes cut, or even ad-libs that made the final cut, you can only judge the final product. Maybe later, should you really fall in love with a course and get to meet the architect, then soak up those "what if" stories about why they finished on a par-3 or did not return the 9th to the clubhouse? Otherwise, focus on how the sequence of holes presents a variety of looks, shots and—cliché alert—using every club in the bag.

VARIETY

> *In planning a golf course there are no fixed rules to which it is compulsory to conform, and the variety which results is one of the greatest charms of the game.*

C.H. ALISON, golf architect

Whether a course is 9, 12 or 18 holes, our needs are no different than those of any other audience in a storytelling medium. We want an arc with developments, hooks and a few twists. It's human nature to crave a middle, a beginning and an end. And unless they are trying to post their personal best scores, everyone expects a grand finish that leaves them wanting more. No one wants to play the golf architectural equivalent of a French art house film that just randomly ends.

Still, not every course needs to be *Citizen Kane*, *Abbey Road* or Game 7. But even with modest land, thin budgets and inevitable restrictions, the person penciling out a collection of golf holes should at least try to inject the design with a blend of distances, changes of direction and bends to the holes. Let's consider why each of these attributes matter, with some often overlooked caveats thrown in for maximum connoisseurship pleasure.

Blend of distances. A little of this, a little of that. *A bottle of red, a bottle of white.* It all depends on your appetite. Trying too hard to give the golfer every single possible hole yardage on canvases ill-suited to covering every conceivable distance, will result in the creation of a formulaic and forced design. The every-club-in-the-bag cliché really does speak to a solidly executed design. Ideally, however, the architect gets to a place of varied distances and shot shapes without anyone noticing. The designer might even pull it off while leaning on their favorite formulas.

One of the most successful architects of all time returned to a set "template" of holes from other courses. While this kind of mimicry could be campy in other arts, Seth Raynor turned to a collection of hole concepts that he built for his boss C.B. Macdonald, who brought them back from Scotland, England and other parts of Europe. Macdonald went with what was, at the risk of sounding disrespectful, a theme-course route during the early days of American golf to show his countrymen how golf architecture could better the burgeoning sport. To do so, Macdonald used the templates to educate golfers about the possibilities of course design when early U.S. courses were ghastly messes complete with coffin-shaped bunkers, chocolate drop mounds and circles of sand masquerading as greens.

Raynor repeatedly relied on the templates to great effect in his solo work. Yet adhering to certain yardages was never part of the template formula. (Though the Short hole needed to be short!). The holes have names like Redan, Biarritz, Road, etc., and have become well known today after going misunderstood for decades. In Raynor's case, he came from an engineering background and was not a golfer. Yet he still managed to inject all sorts of new ideas, twists and original elements into his "covers" despite never having seen the originals. Like Ray Charles covering "Georgia On My Mind," Raynor often improved on the originals. He did not rigidly adhere to set distances or features. Despite this formulaic rehashing in all his designs, Raynor courses also feel fresh, memorable and worthwhile even as he played the same songs wherever he took the stage.

The original par-3 15th at North Berwick (above) was named the Redan for a type of fortress and spawned multiple offshoots despite playing as an awkward hole with limited visibility of the flagstick. One of the most prominent examples can be found on the 4th hole at National Golf Links of America. (Geoff Shackelford)

Long after Raynor, plenty of other architects approached design with far less imagination and got caught up in the quest to achieve perfect variety. As 7,000 yards and par-72 became American stamps of design approval, the quest for organic variety took a back seat to reaching certain overall distances and course ratings. In the late 20th century, course-ranking lists came along and drove design values. And, when "Variety" was added as a voting category for panelists, most architects, knowing how their bread was buttered, responded by playing to the rankings by increasingly over-prioritizing perceived variety in their designs. Unfortunately, most of the greatest early designs would fail variety tests based on a scorecard study, no matter how much golfers say they used "every club in the bag."

Now, before you open an Excel spreadsheet and enter the course yardages to analyze the variety of distances and pars, make sure the generic numbers are not deceiving. I've seen plenty of holes with similar distances play in very different ways. Especially par-4s and par-5s. If you've been lucky enough to play Pebble Beach, you know the 8th, 9th and 10th holes present three long par-4s in a row. But no one would scold the architect for redundancy because the golfer gets to play three epic cliffside holes, each with distinctive touches and character.

Par-3s are a different beast. Whether you're a new player or one of the world's best golfers, few things announce design laziness more than a set of one-shotters playing the same distance and direction. A similar set of threes is almost never a set of four short shots. You know, the kind every golfer loves for those wily do-or-die qualities where an entire foursome can have a shot at glory.

No matter how many times we hear how everyone loves a shortish par-3, they don't seem to happen often enough. Blame the formula-loving accountants. Shortish par-3s drag down the scorecard quest to get a course

Pebble Beach's 8th, 9th and 10th holes are all long par-4s but each has distinctive qualities that allows such a lack of variety to work. (Google Earth)

over a distance figure that a marketing-minded developer demands (usually 7,000 yards). So we often get four par-3s of 205 yards, easily the least interesting distance for a one-shotter. Playing a course with four or more of these is the golf equivalent of an album full of six-minute ballads about death.

Another authenticity killer often sold in the name of variety: the modern addiction to par-70 or higher. The overall par has nothing to do with our enjoyment of the sport and no one really knows why the number must start with a seven or else a course is not of "championship" variety, and it is true that only one major has been played under a par of 70. But the determined effort to land on a number starting with 7 can lead to forced par-4s or par-5s when the topography might have been better suited to a short par-4, followed by a short par-3 that might have produced a par-70 or, horror of all horrors and the end of humanity as we know it, a par-69.

No matter what kind of restrictions are faced in creating a course, the golf architect should at least try for one short par-3 under 140 yards, a

The short 17th hole at Sand Hills viewed from the 100-yard tee. The hole maxes out at 146 yards. (Geoff Shackelford)

medium length shot around 170, another in that morbidly depressing ballad distance of 205 yards (if you must), and a long one that isn't a total buzzkill to play. (Some of the greatest par-3s in golf are long and with an extra back tee might turn the hole into a fun short par-4.)

But retaining Normalcy remains the priority. So please, no spreadsheets, graphs, white-boarding or other time-wasting efforts to check off a perfect variety of distances. In judging the routing's memorability, simply take note of distances but also make sure not to penalize a place for a perceived imbalance when character, cool landforms, and fun holes seem to present something a little different. Maybe even perfect imperfection.

Change of direction. A series of straight, parallel fairways is not the stuff of design dreams. You can and should protest such laziness. Monotonous back and forth holes show about as much vision as a symmetrical grid of residential streets laid out with forgettable names. No matter how many times you visit, the layout is one giant blur where you get lost.

Masterfully designed housing developments share some of the same traces of mystery and unpredictability as golf course routings. They work with the land instead of fighting it. The most seamlessly routed courses are nestled among features and do not require excessive amounts of signage to tell us where to go next. (Seeing an array of arrows telling where the next tee is might be a giveaway that the routing has little of the flowing adventurousness that appeals most.)

Golfers also value the twists, turns and changes in playing corridors for very utilitarian purposes; namely, reducing long stretches of holes playing into the sun or wind. The most "perfectly imperfect" routing from this perspective is found at Muirfield in Scotland. The golfer never heads in the same direction for more than two holes in a row. This magnificent links presents every type of shot imaginable. Memorability comes easy. The par-3s play in different directions. And it's all so balanced on paper that someone could accuse the place of trying too hard. Yet a stroll with clubs would never give a sense of over-engineered variety by the architects who made it into a masterpiece (first ballot Golf Architecture Hall of Famers Old Tom Morris, H.S. Colt and Tom Simpson). Only when you step back, map out the sequencing and pick apart Muirfield without clubs, does its completeness become apparent.

Blend of bends. A mix in the degrees of hole twists and turns, a.k.a. doglegs, will distinguish a place even if the other design features are bland. Depending on how architects incorporate natural tilts and elevation changes, they will ideally present a sound combination of holes bending left, some veering right, a few that play straight and a few taking a hard turn. Creating a serpentine effect should not be a tall ask unless building on a mountainside. There is also an intangible excitement inspired by holes imploring us to play toward a spot which, when we do, rewards us with the

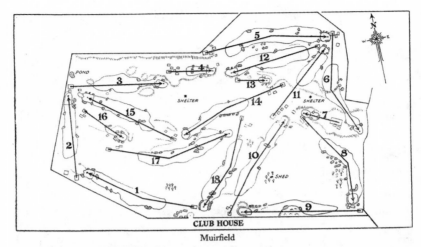

Muirfield

The "perfect" routing of Muirfield changes directions and subjects players to a variety of the elements compared to an "out and back" sequence.

next shot opening up gloriously at position-A, around the dogleg corner with an inviting look at the green. It's akin to rounding a building-lined city street and revealing a grand scene. Paris does this well with the Eiffel Tower.

An architect also addresses questions of bias toward certain shot shapes when mixing up the curvature of holes. A course with only dogleg rights is almost guaranteed to be panned the way a chef would be for putting chicken on a starter, salad and entrée. Jack Nicklaus can attest to how golfers feel about even the slightest bias. His fellow pros believed he designed with his high, left-to-right shot shape in mind. They may not have been entirely wrong. He heard the criticism and probably quietly grumbled: *No I'm the greatest player ever and could play anything, so stop your whining.* But he listened and probably overcompensated for this perceived bias later in his career.

So when judging a course with an apparent excess of holes curving in that unfortunate direction, make sure to note the design touches within all those dogleg rights. The architect may have known this was an issue and tried to offset it with features calling upon wildly different tee shots. Perhaps a few of those right-bending holes reward a left-to-right drive hugging the dogleg. But a few of those might call on a safe lay-up down the left side and an inverse shot shape from the tee to set up the best look. And practice patience, young Jedis. These nuances can take a while to discover.

STICKY-BUT-SURMOUNTABLE IDEAS

A designer knows he has achieved perfection not when there is nothing left to add, but when there is nothing left to take away.
ANTOINE de SAINT-EXUPÉRY

Anyone with a budget can make a two-hour movie full of car chases, shoot-outs, explosions and clichéd dialogue. A writer can pile up the bodies in a mystery. A cook can throw every fresh ingredient imaginable into a pot and make something taste just fine. It's called a stew.

Given a decent budget and an edict to turn farmland into a world beater, golf architects have been known to throw their version of celery, carrots, onions, herbs, spices and stock around to create a golf course full of special effects. But the layouts thriving over time did not prioritize bold first impressions at the expense of playability, affordability or nature. Other than some high-end resort courses with aspirations of charging $500, golf courses should be designed for repeat fun. Yet to crave playing somewhere again and again, we need design ideas to stick enough to make us work without demoralizing our spirit. No one wants to be plastered in carbonite like Han Solo.

This final piece to the memorability puzzle is the most complex, debated and subjective. It goes like this: Does the course present evocative design touches that you can overcome without emptying your bag of $4 golf balls?

Maybe a lone pot bunker at the dogleg corner tempts you into a bold carry due to its pitifully minuscule size, making it easily avoidable. Or the effect is the total opposite. A huge fairway bunker defines the look from the tee, but, once past the yawning beast, you are rewarded with an easy pitch to the green. The more these sticky hazards tempt rather than discourage, toy instead of murder and tease rather than torture, the more memorable they become.

Sticky, but surmountable features.

Other times, the architect may present you with something unexpected. Say, a natural creek bisecting the fairway at 400 yards. This oddity is not within reach but adds pressure to the tee shot. Smack a good one or else you'll face an ego-deflating decision whether to lay-up short of the creek. This feature, merely caused by Mother Nature needing to collect water and take it somewhere else, sticks.

Then there are the even more nuanced design touches that add to the stickiness calculus. For example, a subtle ridge bisects a green. This seemingly minor feature in the grand scheme of 150 acres or more, entrenches deep in your cranium once you three-putted from the wrong side. But this little ridge also gets you thinking back at tee where you now must note the hole location. Perhaps today's cup rewards a tee shot down the left side so you don't have to play over this simple feature, one that might bound your ball over the back edge. Holding the green becomes tougher from the right and you will have to live with the regret for hours to come after having not hit a nice draw down the left side.

Sticky but surmountable features do not draw blood. But they can stick in your craw.

As much as the sequence and diversity of holes can matter, noticing and remembering these subtle brushstrokes will charm your sensibilities the more you play a course. You'll also score better noticing these details.

No course...should be so obvious as to reveal itself upon one viewing. Any course worth the effort of construction should have enough nuances of character and strategy to hold the players' interest and maintain a sense of mystery and discovery over a long period.

BILL COORE, golf architect

A golf course is not supposed to torture. Its life will likely be short-lived or one of loneliness if created only as an afterthought to a development of townhouses in the high 900s. The best courses enhance the landscape. The worst announce their presence too loudly. Even the world's best golfers get this. Notice what they say the next time a big tournament visits an older course built in the early 20th century. They're always smitten with what a nice "walk in the park" it offers. And how the place "looks like it's always been there," or how great it is that "anyone can play this" so "why can't we have more courses like this?"

Conversely, we have too many bloated 18-holers that are those flat films you'd never want to watch again. Like a stupidly expensive steakhouse you might try on special occasions, these are not the neighborhood joints with reliable home-cooked specials. Increasingly, golfers are coming around to appreciating a tried and true course, especially if it's fun and does not charge exorbitantly stiff green fees. The cool kids value a course people like playing again and again.

The par-5 4th hole (Klondyke) at Lahinch features a distinct ridge in the green to emphasize different attack angles depending on the hole location. (Cameron Hurdus)

That sound of golfers laughing and cheering a great shot?

Yes!

Joyous laughing heard throughout the course to the annoyance of the Smails foursome?

Yes, sir!

Par-3 courses and low-key fun to make an awkward game more welcoming or to restore your faith after a tough day on the big course?

Hipster approved!

There is very little repeat fun in trying break 100 on a course with a 74.5 rating. Designs are at their most appealing when trouble can be overcome. We don't want eighteen songs played so loud you can't take the club back without trembling. Or courses full of features to stop us from occasionally beating an architect who wasn't hugged enough as a child. Golfers will always be drawn to old school ideas offered by a blend of subtle, quirky cool and forgiving. Sticky but surmountable.

This is all a fancy way of saying the most memorable and satisfying holes always come down to risks surmountable enough that you want to take them on again and again. The art of presenting perilous situations, while letting a golfer occasionally declare little victories, may be the toughest task for architects to achieve. The stickiest ideas we treasure require time, patience, creativity and a healthy ego on behalf of a designer to dangle carrots before ultimately presenting situations where shrewd golfers can overcome obstacles. Finding such a balance differentiates courses we merely remember from those we want to play Every Day.

Chapter 4

E FOR EVERY DAY:
COULD YOU PLAY THE COURSE
EVERY DAY AND NEVER TIRE OF IT?

Experience, playability and strategic intrigue

A good golf course makes you want to play so badly you hardly have time to change your shoes.

BEN CRENSHAW, golfer and course architect

It's a simple question capable of unfurling layers of nuance and emotion. But it's also the most straightforward way to sort through hype, bunker schemes and everything else about a course to reveal what really matters.

Could you play the course Every Day and never tire of it?

This is far different from a seemingly similar question of architectural introspection that we might ask while standing in a line buying lotto tickets and dreaming of what one course, given unlimited resources, freedom of choice and the upgrade in bloodlines after winning the Powerball: Given only one option, what course would I chose to play every day the rest of my life? (This bucket list version of the question is fleshed out in Chapter 6.)

Our E for Every Day seeks to precisely target what it is about the kooky confection of experience, fun, intrigue and playability separating the Every Days from the On Occasion courses. The Every Day subject asks us to dig just deep enough to identify the courses with the stickiest ideas everyone enjoys tackling, while weeding out those only inducing weariness or all-out misery. But the question is vulnerable to emotions and biases that cannot be ignored. So in a stubbornly realized concession to reality and topped off with light shavings of guilt, I'll just say it: Experience matters.

Not the old-age kind. The *how does this place make me feel* type of experience.

While this acknowledgment may lead to book burnings of *Golf Architecture for Normal People* at the next Donald Ross Society meeting, we all connect to courses offering just enough spirit of discovery and adventure to keep us coming back, warts and all. Maybe it's walkable and set in a nice enough landscape that soothes the soul. It's your happy place.

No course can attain the Every Day blue check mark if it's dreary to visit or consistently under maintained or exuding a vibe that says: We just want to take your money. Surrounding experience elements can drive the desire to answer yes to the Every Day question and it's silly to ignore them. Because sometimes, as Ben Crenshaw said, the place makes you so eager to put your shoes on and rush out the door. And it's not just those artsy bunkers or fun, short par-4s that offer a well-deserved respite from the grind.

Beyond this element of the Every Day experience, the course still has to offer playability and strategic factors and we'll explore those as well. But first, let's look at the ways the course experience influences perception and the best ways to manage the most emotional aspect of the Every Day query.

IDEAL DESIGNS VS. IDEAL ADVENTURES

Playing around a golf course is not merely a question of getting around, like traveling over a race course or walking around the block. It's rather a question of taking nine or eighteen separate and distinct little journeys, each of which presents its own distinct pictures and its own distinct problems as part of the grand tour.

CHARLES BANKS

Two of my favorite courses sit in a beautiful area called East Lothian outside Edinburgh. While previously cited Muirfield is rightfully touted as the most complete design in this hallowed region, two other nearby links are my very favorite places to play golf. These courses pass the Every Day test with flying colors: North Berwick's West Links and Gullane Nos. 1, 2 or 3. And they share very little in common except adjacent postal codes.

North Berwick is wild, weird and, over recent years, increasingly tapped by many as their favorite course in Scotland and beyond. The West Links starts off in the beach town of North Berwick. Like many typical Scottish courses, the first hole and 18th share a fairway. They are probably the two least interesting on the course, though they're both still sensational holes. From there, North Berwick features some of the zaniest holes on the planet. It's been a vital inspiration for most architects. Budding designers still use it as an outdoor masterclass, just as C.B. Macdonald and others did in studying the par-3 Redan over a century ago.

North Berwick's seemingly simpler holes get better the more you play them, while the zany stuff only becomes more thrilling once you embrace hitting shots over walls, on grassy dunes or into preternatural greens. The course routing takes you to a very far point before returning home. But changes in pace and character mean the West Links routing will never get slapped with the sometimes unflattering "out and back" moniker. The course builds to a big, dramatic finish with a string of countless features worthy of rigorous banter over a post-round pint. North Berwick is perfectly imperfect. To go with its collection of zany holes, the West Links exudes an adventurous sensibility. The same goes for Gullane, right down the road.

> *Having played Gullane No. 2 in the morning and No. 1 in the afternoon, my mind is an agreeable jumble between the two. There is, of course, a strong family likeness between the two because on both we have (like the grand Old Duke of York of the poem) to march up to the top of the hill and march down again. The marching up at the second hole on No. 1 and the third hole on No. 2 is desperate work, but once we are at the top, the golf on both courses is most engaging and good sound golf as well. The marching down in each case to the 17th is good fun enough, involving a cheerful joy shot and the thought of a little refreshment.*
>
> BERNARD DARWIN, golf writer

The three-courses at Gullane start in a charming town facing a giant and alarmingly mundane-looking hill. It's hardly a textbook canvas for golf and one most modern architects would have passed on or rearranged to make it seem less like a golf course playing over a forgettable hill. Portions of all three Gullane layouts eventually play on sandy, bumpy linksland just like

The West Links' first and 18th holes returning to the town of North Berwick. (David Jones)

North Berwick, but set just a bit higher above the sea and offering glorious views. That's about where the similarities end.

Gullane's three courses take you on a singular adventure. You climb the hill, experience thrilling shots and culminate with life-affirming views, before trundling down toward town again. The courses somehow overcome a prominent design feature most people loathe—playing steeply uphill. The emotions tapped by Gullane, however, are utterly distinct from those stirred by North Berwick.

More connected to the quaint town of Gullane, a round is jump-started by the golf-friendly atmosphere. Not that North Berwick is hostile to the game. It's just that the golf in Gullane starts on the main street. Consequently, you can walk down the street with your clubs, plus-fours, a big fluffy ball atop your driving cap, and somehow, not feel the least bit ashamed. Whether the first time playing there or the one hundredth, playing up the hill is packed with anticipation knowing special holes await. But you also better not take those openers lightly. And in drier years, the steeply downhill finishing holes are absurdly fun. Just get the ball on its way, then stand back, arms akimbo, and marvel as it careens and meanders on it way, nearly frictionless, trundling on for a hundred yards or more before finally finding a resting spot.

Add to this frame views of the rocky Berwick Law hill overlooking North Berwick in the distance, and, on a clear day, Arthur's Seat in Edinburgh, and a round at Gullane becomes an expedition. At this vantage, you have walked into a living history of the sport. So inspiring it makes the thought of hitting a ball (almost) moot.

The courses, especially No. 1, reaffirm your faith in something grander than yourself and make you happy to come back to climb the hill again. But are the courses at Gullane a design lab worthy of intense study? With holes as identifiable world-beaters that would land on lists of the greatest holes alongside the best of North Berwick? Nope.

But weave it all together and the experience is satisfying in ways no design criteria can address.

> *The charm of the seaside courses of Great Britain lies in their multiformity, their unconventionality, their infinite variety. There are eighteen holes, and the yardage is up to standard, but comparison largely ends there. The terrain itself has an individuality all its own. In its uneven diversity, its tumbling irregularity, its unrivalled originality, linksland bears no resemblance to any other territory.*
>
> ROBERT HUNTER

We all know the golfer who places excess importance on his or her scores or vanity-driven stuff like the pyramids of ProV1s at the Practice

The 18th green (right) and first tee with the adjacent town of Gullane. (David Jones)

Area (capitalized!), double-cut greens in August and a grand piano player on the range (oh, it's a thing). Such golfers love their pomp, circumstance and heavy schmoozing and are unable to weigh how these X factors impact a course's Every Day palatability.

We all get how Trent and Brent greet you in the parking lot with your clubs, an ice-cold bottle of spring water from the Ouachita mountains, a sleeve of Pro V1s and a towel waiting for you in your cart. And yes, those earnest cart barn boys cleansed your clubs overnight of demons. They even mention how you've never looked slimmer. Eventually, Trent and Brent will move on to another job. So that lavish service they provide to the point you might answer Yes to the Every Day question, despite the course wearing you out most days, is fleeting.

We all get how an incredible driving range with a saccharine short game area floats boats. Or how the lushly landscaped entrance drive takes on Babylonian vibes as you wonder what lot in life gave you access to such

The view high above Gullane Hill, where golfers play back toward the charming town. (David Jones)

posh theatrics. Then there are all the maintenance touches prone to make the experience enchanting. Maybe it's how the greenkeeper stripes the fairways to look amazing for your guests, even if you're paying mightily for the effect or tight lies are tougher to hit from than a fairway kept a few millimeters longer. Or how the bunkers and the bright white sand trucked in from Nova Scotia never give you a bad lie.

Which reminds me: Today's superintendents are the unsung heroes of golf's survival in its 21st-century resurgence. They deliver widespread quality with more sustainable practices than at any time in golf's long history. The sheer number of days they present their courses in good to great shape is often taken for granted. Try to remember this when asking them why the greens weren't cut today or when seizing on some other factor that might unfairly start to seep into your Every Day assessment.

Bear in mind that a comfortable, clean movie theater featuring amazing sound and popcorn will improve the film-viewing experience. But those factors will never overcome a lousy story with mailed-in performances. And even the most astute panelists struggle to evaluate a course after the greens have been punched or playing on a day with winds so strong they could not tell whether the holes were well designed. The very best raters will sometimes even admit how their score turned an unbiased assessment into a selfish one. So in running the Every Day question through your mental servers, I humbly ask that you consider which experiential elements were fleeting, and which embellish your enjoyment of the design.

PLAYABILITY: OLD RELIABLES VS. ROLLERCOASTER RIDES

A golf hole, humanly speaking, is like life, in as much as one cannot judge justly of any person's character the first time one meets him. Sometimes it takes years to discover and appreciate hidden qualities which only time discloses, and he usually discloses them on the links.

C.B. MACDONALD

Is the layout challenging but not overwhelmingly difficult?

Those eight words seem like a safe barometer for nearly all courses. But dark forces love to swoop in and replace "challenging" with "fair," a swap that almost immediately rewards a bland design. And to the smaller subset of architects charged with building daily fee courses for a large audience, playability has often meant a course devoid of interesting bunkers or a hint of slope in the greens. It's as if the design had only one purpose: to herd golfers like cattle instead of providing design zest for the betterment of lives and the enhancement of landscape.

Thanks to links golf, we know the sport grew mainly because the early golf courses provided enough obstacles with multiple routes for getting around the trouble. Coping with hazards and unpredictability added to the charm. Back in the days when breaking 95 made you the elite of the elite, golfers were drawn to weaving around and over hazards. They identified with fun and not the score they would be posting for handicap purposes.

The golf architect's toughest task has always been in finding the yin and yang between forgiveness and intrigue. They're usually trying to appease golfers of all skill levels, while often needing to make every course tournament worthy for ego or marketing reasons. But as numerous beloved designs have proven, balancing challenge with an Every Day level of fun can be done. Nearly all of golf architecture's most timeless works find a way to satisfy the largest number of golfers possible. Right now, architectural elitists are contesting: "But George Crump didn't pander to all players with Pine Valley! It's a macho, manly and brutally difficult course with 18 incredible holes that only the elites can handle!"

The perennial No. 1 American design on most lists sets out to be different. Every hole was to be epic. And it aspired to be what it, in fact, became: a non-stop rollercoaster ride. You can even stop at the amusement park just outside the property line if you want a preview of the thrills to come. But even Crump's original ideas needed massaging after Pine Valley's rough-and-tumble formative years. The ambitious design suffered setbacks and took time to develop. Crump passed away before all 18 were in play. But when this masterpiece first opened for limited play, some of his more radical ideas needed massaging by architect H.S. Colt and members who later became notable dabblers in golf architecture.

Their goal in "tweaking" Pine Valley? Deliver more function and less form.

They made Pine Valley more playable.

Today, even with advancements in technology and modern day manicuring of its once ferocious sandy scrub areas, Pine Valley is still a refined amusement park ride of emotions and heroic shots. The same could be said for Bethpage State Park's infamous

The original 18th green at Pine Valley as seen in an advertisement. A "pimple" in the green was soon removed, proving that even the masterpieces are not perfect from the start.

Black Course, which even comes with an infamous warning sign now made into merchandise.

—WARNING—
The Black Course Is An Extremely Difficult Course Which We Recommend ONLY for Highly Skilled Golfers

The Black is technically "playable," it's just not much fun if you try to post a decent score. But the architects knew the facility would have other playing options (there are five 18-hole courses) and designed each with varying degrees of difficulty.

There's a fine line with playability. Thankfully, the Every Day question's "never tire of it" clause has a knack for narrowing down the places combining enough surprise and suspense without overdoing it. The courses we want to play Every Day present solvable, satisfying puzzles leaving us wanting more.

So what is the St. Peter's Basilica of great golf courses? The umami of golf architecture? That ultimate "never tire of" ingredient you can find on the simplest muni all the way up to Pine Valley?

AN INTELLIGENT PURPOSE

The object of golf architecture is to give an intelligent purpose to the striking of a golf ball. To be worthwhile, this purpose must excite and hold interest. If it fails in this, the character of the architecture is at fault.

MAX BEHR, golf architect

The "intelligent purpose" that Max Behr argues for is at once obvious and elusive: Has the architect repeatedly prompted the player to ask:

"Why?"

Or "Should I?"

Or "What if?"

Maybe a bunker off the tee must be carried to give the next shot a wide-open approach. Play safe and the angle or view on the next shot positively stinks.

Or the designer presents a diagonal row of bunkers that sure looks like a cruel way to gobble up golf balls. Yet he also offers a handsome reward for taking an aggressive line to take a longer path to the hole.

Sometimes that diagonal hazard really does just gobble up golf balls and creates misery. That's penal design.

The more you play, the less a smorgasbord of irrelevant hazards impresses when you grasp how little intrigue they hold, and how little utility they serve despite the heavy cost to maintain them. They are self-indulgent folly. But when you discover holes where the architect injected an intelligent purpose and tempted you to try a shot just beyond your normal abilities? One rewarding a combo platter of brains, brawn and courage? There may be no better feeling than when confronted with such conundrums, making the right decision and pulling off the shot. It's a win-win for the designer and golfer alike.

To create timeless strategic holes requires good ingredients, early prep work in the kitchen, careful testing to make sure the flavors complement one another and cohesive presentation by the plating team and wait staff (the maintenance crew in this latest food analogy). The best holes are driven by one seemingly silly little feature that holds repercussions far and wide. Close your eyes and search through those vast mental archives you've amassed of favorite holes. I bet when you pick apart your favorite courses, you can name a key feature distinguishing each hole. Maybe it's a big bump in the middle of the second green. Those cross bunkers off the fourth tee. Or some kind reprieve from the tediousness of every landing area pinched by a bunker-left and bunker-right scheme that is the epitome of lazy design.

Also key to Every Day strategy: the smaller the better. Either via placement, optical illusions, or the ability to make you uncomfortable. The tinier the feature, the more infuriating it is that we let it mess with our play. The annoyance factor is compounded because there was so much room to avoid the trouble. Things like a natural mound, an easily avoidable pot bunker or a crafty tilt to the green are often all the architect needs to spark strategy-induced angst. We imagine it could be dangerous so, therefore, it becomes excessively dangerous.

Anyone can design a hole that looks better suited to one of those zany world's toughest hole calendars. The real artist creates something with just enough character to tempt us to engage again and again. The more mysterious the better. And nothing is more satisfying than watching an average player who knows his or her limitations, play smart and beat the flat-bellied, scratch golfer who bragged about his TrackMan combine scores and takes the overly ambitious route.

When our natural golf curiosity is left with few or no questions to answer due to an out-sized scale and an everything-but-the-kitchen-sink approach, the courses become a deafening cacophony. Were there ten bunkers on that hole? Eleven? Did any of them make me think about my options? Or was the only task to avoid all the trouble? When an architect comes at you this way, hole after hole, the excess becomes conspicuously distracting, and, at some point, we make a mental note never to play the course again.

The best strategic courses also have a flair for the cinematic. So much of a design's stickiness depends on how a collection of holes work together, keep you guessing and build to a big finish. Some courses peak before the last stretch because the clubhouse is far from the most dramatic land. But even in those situations, the best productions lure you in and layer on the strategic questions as the course goes. The best architects rarely serve the main course first. The elements of memorability and playability crystalize as the course builds to something grand.

Spyglass Hill is the ultimate case study in opening with the climactic scenes, making return trips even less exciting. The course essentially opens with the light saber fight to decide whether good staves off evil.

Built on a scenic hill overlooking the Pacific and inside the 17-Mile Drive, the course starts with holes in the dunes before finishing with the final 14 in a lovely Monterey Pine forest. But by starting through the most dramatic and appetizing land for golf, the grandeur of the tree-lined holes becomes a letdown. Had the course been flipped—starting in the trees and finishing in the dunes—the curiosity factor would have been ascending. Each hole might have been more subtle knowing a big reveal was looming. Instead, it's just very, very hard and light on strategy. As Jack Nicklaus famously said, "Pebble Beach and Cypress Point make you want to play golf. Spyglass makes you want to go fishing."

STRATEGIC VS. PENAL

The strategic belief is providing alternatives, highlighting positional play, recognizing the ability to flight the ball, encouraging guile and ingenuity, and rewarding risk. The punishment must fit the crime. Good architects tempt and tease not torment. Subtlety and sympathy are the substance of strategy.

DONALD STEEL

It would be cruel at this point to delve deep into the rabbit hole of past design debates over the merits of strategic versus penal design. I'll keep it brief. But first a key clarification: it's pronounced pēn(ə)l . Not pēn(ī)l. You'll thank me later.

At various points throughout golf history, design practitioners have come along believing their job is to rearrange the earth and to penalize every miss in some big way. Maybe they were misanthropes unloved as children? We'll never know. In any case, people kept hiring them even when it was proven repeatedly that their courses were no fun. Don't try to figure it out.

The opposing school of thought believed in only massaging the terrain to incentivize risk-taking and to subsequently reward a good shot. They were inspired by the Old Course, where the riskier tee shot placement sets up a better angle for the next shot. Or, sometimes, the risk-taker gained a better view of the target compared to the person who played safe from the tee. Strategy.

The key difference between these schools of design comes down to punishment. Strategic architects allow you to play safe, but you also must accept some inconvenience for having taken that easy way out. However, if you, the bullish golfer, decide today you must attack and choose the riskier

Small features can wreak havoc far and wide, like this pot bunker at Rustic Canyon's 13th. (Geoff Shackelford)

shot, just know the strategic architect will make you work for it but will reward success. The penal designer hopes every shot is hard work for every golfer. His design incentivizes survival. Inspiration is squelched to keep you in line. Obedience rules in the penal design school. And this is where you are probably wondering: How come architects do not inject strategy into every hole they create?

Some architects try. Sometimes options are ruined by course changes or maintenance conditions. Options require width, but if yardage is the priority, acreage goes to length and that precious landing area space is compromised. Stretch a rubber band to see how this works.

Inspiring curiosity without giving all the secrets away can be quite tricky. Golfers generally want a big first impression and few questions left

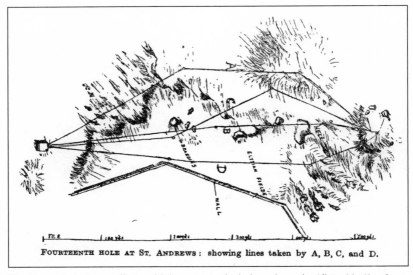

FOURTEENTH HOLE AT ST. ANDREWS : showing lines taken by A, B, C, and D.

The 14th at St Andrews offers multiple routes to the hole as drawn by Alister MacKenzie. The ultimate in strategic design even if it largely happened by accident. (Alister MacKenzie)

after they step onto a tee. Your C.B. Macdonalds, Alister MacKenzies, George Thomases and A.W. Tillinghasts—knew how to do this while building holes that held up on repeat playing. They could also layer their stories with emotion, nuance, surprises and thought-provoking scenes you'll want to relive again and again. A few artists take pride in building holes with such a deep sense of the unknown that only they fully understand the genius of their architectural means and methods. Some of their adherents insist tactical reasons lie under profound layering only the wisest observers can locate. Yet the greatest architects always found a place in between mysterious and over-the-top.

    Unlike other interactive art forms, the golf architect is remodeling Earth. The architect faces a different level of responsibility in working with

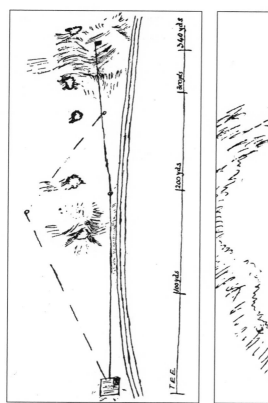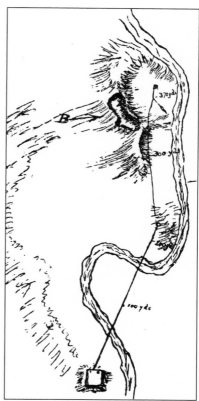

Two sketches by Alister MacKenzie highlighting classic strategy. The safe play away from the trouble leaves a less favorable angle for the next shot to the green. This type of classic strategy creates Every Day fun for all levels of golfer. Each rewards tee shots flirting with trouble by creating an easier second shot.

a canvas already created over millennia by Mother Nature. Architects need to show respect and take care when injecting the sticky but surmountable touches. Otherwise, their creation will fail to hold up over time.

This is why the greatest design practitioners deliberated over the essence of strategic vs. penal design. And why they always celebrated holes incorporating natural features instead of over-manufacturing the landscape. They idolized the old masters and only sought to embellish nature with deft brushstrokes.

The best architects today continue to grapple with the question of design endurance, constantly trying to grasp why some holes stand the test of time while others needed constant redesign. They wanted to make you laugh and even sometimes cry in delight. They wanted their courses to entertain. Every. Day.

Chapter 5

D FOR DOG FRIENDLINESS: A COURSE WHERE YOU'D TAKE A DOG FOR A WALK

Scale, walkability, drainage and natural beauty

> *The poor dog, in life the firmest friend,*
> *The first to welcome, foremost to defend,*
> *Whose honest heart is still his master's own,*
> *Who labors, fights, lives, breathes for him alone.*
>
> LORD BYRON

You see, Greg, when you yell at a dog, his tail will go between his legs and cover his genitals, his ears will go down. A dog is very easy to break, but cats make you work for their affection. They don't sell out the way dogs do.

JACK BYRNES, the protagonist of *Meet the Parents*

Young caddie, Freddie Tait and Nails by J.H. Lorimer. This portrait was commissioned by R&A members after Tait's death in the Boer War. Reproduced by kind permission of The Royal and Ancient Golf Club of St Andrews.

A long time ago in a golf galaxy far, far away, no one used to think much of our four-legged friends serving as integral golf companions. Early golf paintings occasionally included a furry friend in the gallery or accompanying noble golfers, dutifully watching and wondering what all the fuss is about.

There may be no more famous portrait of player and pet than legendary amateur golfer Freddie Tait, who was known to bring "Nails" along for many of his rounds. A terrier "in every inch and every pound of his 35-lb. body," according to early golf observer John Low, Nails sometimes wondered off in search of trouble, only to resurface at dinner time. He could be "hard company," sources say.

Nails was fiercely loyal and integral to his master's success. Tait even trained "his son" to forecaddie and find lost balls. When Tait attempted the outlandish feat of breaking 40 playing shots from Royal St George's to Royal Cinque Port's clubhouse, a stretch of open linksland separated the courses and required Nails's nose. Since a dog's sense of smell is estimated to be millions of times more sensitive than ours, the wee pooch had no trouble deciphering his owner's gutta percha. Sadly, there are no YouTube videos of the feat. Spoiler alert: Tait's 32nd stroke went through a Royal Cinque Port's upstairs window. There's still no word on who paid for the broken window. Today, homes obstruct Tait's route, though some noble golfers still pay tribute to the feat by playing from one course to the other, only along the beach when the tide is out.

While away at the Second Boer War, the thirty-year-old Tait asked for updates on his little friend. When Tait died at Koodoosberg, fellow soldiers found a small "Dear Father" letter from Nails in his pocket. The signature was a paw print.

Pausing here to let you wipe away tears.

Boys and their Dog Playing Musselburgh Links. (William Douglas, 1809) Reproduced by kind permission of The Royal and Ancient Golf Club of St Andrews.

Nails became so central to Tait's legacy that the terrier was included in a John Henry Larimer portrait still hanging in a prime R&A clubhouse location overlooking the 18th at the Old Course. This despite nefarious, unsubstantiated rumors that the wee terrier was banished from St Andrews for fighting with another canine. So why was Nails allowed to wander where he pleased and what does this have to do with sniffing out good golf architecture? Patience! You're learning valuable golf history!

For starters, Freddie Tait was an imposing figure. He stood six feet tall, swam and dove off Step Rock in St Andrews, played rugby and hit

Bust of Greyfriars Bobby outside the cemetery he visited daily and the pub named in his honor. (Geoff Shackelford)

the ball prodigious distances. The masterful St Andrews painter, Thomas Hodge, portrayed Tait in a loincloth at the beach and kicking for a goal. He was a stud. The personable Tait also played a wicked bagpipe and even had a role in Her Majesty's Guard. He became the first to break 70 on the Old Course, often playing five rounds in a day, once drove the 13th green nearly 400 yards away and was one of the U.K.'s best amateur golfers. Old Tom Morris, the preeminent figure and "grandfather" of St Andrews, took Tait under his wing, as did all the town. So much so that he was often thought to be a native son. Another fan was early golf rector John Low, who published a biography of the fallen soldier before the one-year anniversary of Tait's

Golfers and their dog at play, Royal St George's Golf Club. (Geoff Shackelford)

death in 1900. Tait remained an amateur in those days when pros were unfairly viewed as the worst degenerates imaginable. Did I mention that Freddie brought his dog to the golf course whenever possible?

Dogs were a big deal during golf's crucial developing years. They were viewed as smart companions with an important role in Scottish life. Not far from St Andrews in Edinburgh, a local police night watchman died in 1858 and after a funeral procession led by his Skye Terrier "Bobby," was buried in Greyfriars Churchyard. Bobby would not leave his owner's grave. The locals decided to build him a small house and every day, when the Edinburgh Castle gun was shot off at 1 p.m., Bobby would venture out to a public house where he was fed, then return to the gravesite. He did this for fourteen years! Bobby became a major attraction, a Disney movie, and is buried just outside the cemetery. Today he has a statue and bar in his honor where admirers flock to pay tribute and boop his (statue) nose.

There is something deeply romantic watching a dog enjoying the freedom to roam. There's no surprise, then, that they love (most) golf courses. It's also little wonder that so many golfers are drawn to the idea of sharing certain natural curiosities with their quadrupedal friends.

> *Walking through the world with her, watching her reactions, I began to imagine her experience. My enjoyment of a narrow winding path in a shady forest, lined with low bushes and grasses, comes in part from seeing how Pump enjoyed it: the cool of the shade, of course, but also the pathiness, allowing her to zoom along unchecked, stopping only for rousing scents along the sides.*
>
> ALEXANDRA HOROWITZ, author of *Inside of a Dog*

Other than cat people and golf course superintendents who loathe diggers but love them for herding unwanted birds, most golfers wish they could take dogs to the golf course. I desperately wanted to set my Bearded Collie Ruggles free to saunter around the dreamiest of these (largely) safe and fun expanses to explore while I played. Only the beach might have excited him more. Which is why Scottish golf courses in the direct path to the Promised Land of sand, sea, chewable driftwood and other playtime pooches, must adhere to the "Scottish Outdoor Access Code" established for the protection of public passageways. So long as dog walkers stay off the greens and out of "games" playing through, they are permitted to cut through the links with a dog on the "lead" (leash). Other than dumb puppies, most veteran dogs know how to act when allowed to roam free.

If you've ever been to Scotland or Ireland, you've witnessed the early morning or late evening sight of dog and owner walking through a course. In England they're even more free to tag along for golf. At some of the

United Kingdom's finest clubs, including several with "Royal" in the title, you'll see dogs welcomed. The late Queen Elizabeth's love of corgis probably helped normalize things. And at some of the seemingly oldest and stuffiest places, you'll see dog treats in the pro shop and water bowls next to on-course drinking fountains. This general hospitality toward dogs may even help non-golfers perceive courses as vital community green spaces instead of unwelcoming, exclusive bastions.

In America? Not so fast. Yet.

Pebble Beach's tolerance for late-afternoon dog walkers has long helped show that dogs are not evil. There is an ever-growing list of places benefiting from dog friendliness (see Appendix). Increasingly, golfers are allowed to bring man's best friend along as long as they meet a few basic rules. Some places have reported revenue increases thanks to the policy, while more once-uptight clubs are even letting their guard down for "Yappy Hour" events. Golf communities once militantly forbidding late afternoon dog walkers are loosening up their enforcement rules as long as they treat the course and golfers with respect. Still, liability laws and the inability of too many owners and communities to agree on basic boundaries will often put dog walking on the no-no list (unless they belong to the course superintendent).

Regarding the question of this chapter—D for Dog Friendliness— the concept initially had nothing to do with highlighting courses featuring relaxed, canine-friendly policies. But as noted in the previous chapter, there is no point in resisting the experiential interpretation of this question if the place welcomes hounds. Just promise not to deduct points at courses banning dogs to keep them from chasing migrating birds, running off a canyon edge or becoming alligator lunch. And if the superintendent says no dogs today because his crew just put down fertilizer or insecticide, heed the warning.

Golfer David Jones and Alfie out on the links. (Clare Jones)

The D in R.E.D came about after I'd spent a week walking a massive tournament course, only to play another course of quaint scale a day after where a particularly entertaining superintendent's dog put on a show roaming about to the delight of golfers. He could not have done so on the big, bulky tournament course. So "D" for Dog came about to address matters of scale, walkability and quiet beauty. Rare is the golfer who loathes those traits. Even more uncommon is the dog passing up a chance to sniff around a place exuding the aforementioned traits. Though it's not always about smells.

Contrary to popular belief, dogs are not totally color-blind. While we upright two-legged types have photoreceptors able to make out blue, red, and green, dogs have only two. Guess which pair of colors they can see? Blue, and, scientists believe, a greenish-yellow like that of a lean links. As

Maxwell, the maintenance yard's dog, was free to move around at Southern Hills Country Club and enjoy getting wet on a summer day. (Geoff Shackelford)

author Alexandra Horowitz writes in her wonderful book, *Inside of a Dog (What Dogs, See, Smell, and Know)*, our four-legged friends experience color most when in the range of blue to green. No wonder canines go nuts at the sight of a tennis ball or a vast field of verdant green turf. Just like humans!

No matter how tirelessly purists will fight for less-fertilized turf in the name of a firm, fast ground game, most golfers will always grow excited by the sight and scents from deep greens. The fresh-cut grass smell is a mixture of oxygenated hydrocarbons known as green leaf volatiles, clinically proven to induce swooning since, in most climates, humans associate the scent with spring, summer and dreamy weekends on a golf course. Presumably dogs enjoy a similar euphoria when setting out on a trek of random discovery, with cushiony, maintained turf under foot, all while triggering sensations

Sometimes a walk to the next tee can be a serene experience that builds anticipation for the next hole, like this one at Formby in England. (Geoff Shackelford)

and senses they would unlikely encounter while on a tight leash padding down a concrete sidewalk.

Golfers are generally drawn to a similar golf course "pathiness," so long as there is limited hill climbing and few blind shots. When you hear someone comment about a course feeling "like it's always been there," even when it's new, this highlights how its design tapped into the same instinctual pleasures that awoke early links golfers drawn to collections of holes meandering, undulating and gently turning through everything from military embankments, horse racetracks or ideally, dunescapes. The least-interrupted adventures allow us to hit a ball, find it, hit it again and sometimes turn corners and reach plateaus to reveal scenes so invigorating they make you want to take out your phone and snap a photo.

Pathiness also speaks to a certain kind of intangible flow found in the most seamlessly routed courses. When our play is spliced up by treks through tunnels, past other tees and across residential streets, a cadence is lost. There are exceptions to these interruptions, like the occasional walk to the next tee through quiet scenery and delivering a much-needed calming balm!

Few golfers of any era have been heard to say, "Gosh, nice place, BUT the walks from greens to tees are so short and easy." Canines wag their tales less frequently when they sniff their way along straight, paved paths free of mystery: they are happier on a golf course's gently free-wheeling passageways. Dogs may not be the smartest problem-solvers, but they do have, well-placed sources confirm, fantastic memories. They remember rough or blisteringly cold ground under their paws. Golfers have similar "under-foot" senses, which will be addressed presently in the sexy discussion of how drainage is handled.

While humans can stand in one place to take in a view, golfers and dogs like to be on the move. Time is limited. There is a ball to advance. We want to absorb all of the sensory overload that a natural, everchanging golf course conjures up. With those principles in mind, let's dig a bit more into time-honored design elements to help decide whether a course passes the D test.

SCALE

Place the golf course on a level plane; have no traps of any kind; let every fairway be flat; the green unprotected and without rolls, let there be rough; nothing between the tee and the green but a perfect fairway, and the green itself absolutely level; and what would be

the result?—a thing without interest or beauty, on which there is
no thrill of accomplishment which is worthwhile; a situation untrue
to tradition, and apart from the spirit of golf as it was given birth
among the rolling sand dunes of Scotland.

GEORGE THOMAS, golf architect

Scale up. Gain scale. Scale the business. *We'll invest if it scales*, etc., bloody, etcetera.

The corporate world and Silicon Valley have hijacked one of the more versatile words in the English language. And for what? To land Series C funding with an algorithm that will make the world a better place. Oh, joy.

Golfers, whether fully aware or not, treasure intimate scale. The kind of coziness unfriendly to greater profits but appreciated if you are carrying fourteen clubs. From beginners to touring pros, cozy and cool scale always wins out over gargantuan and gaudy. Most golfers do not realize this until exposed to a tight course nestled within a small property that still somehow manages to feel big. Creating this sensibility, while still designing a safe course, is no easy task and one that becomes more complicated the wider misses might fly.

Course design has been through several phases hostile to human and dog pathiness. For a time in the 1970s and 80s, the excessive infatuation with every hole as "a thing unto itself" led to heavy tree planting on existing courses. Or excessive mound-building meant to space out new designs. This separation obsession was mysteriously deemed essential to shielding golfers from other like-minded souls also engaging in the royal and ancient pastime of golf. The fad was fueled by a weird blend of increased liability concerns and top-ranked Pine Valley's tree-lined presentation (even though its site was originally cleared by the architect to open up vistas). The attraction of playing through tight corridors is the golf equivalent of watching TV on a 20-inch screen instead of 55-incher with surround sound. Many courses have since removed the excess encroaching on the original design, thereby unveiling vistas while retaining trees for safety purposes. The result is not only enhanced views, but also increased playability (and fewer lost balls). Several found that they highlighted attractive specimen trees and other land features lost in the clutter. Still, the enjoyment of finding your ball and playing often took an architectural back seat to the weird privacy fad.

Scale took an even greater hit as the sport built courses to accommodate advances in the golf ball and, more recently, all technology. With misses going more sideways and causing unimagined safety issues, the adjusting of average courses to keep up with the Joneses also chipped away at the simple pleasure of walking off a green and on to the next tee 15 yards away.

The pinnacle of excess came at one public course developed to host a U.S. Open. An unlisted set of tees stretched it to over 8,300 yards. The rural course covers most almost 600 acres and is a 5.5 mile walk on a straight line from tees to greens. Somehow, the farthest point from the clubhouse is 2.2 miles away at the 16th hole, about double the longest imaginable "out and back" routing. Erin Hills is not a place to bring Snoopy.

Another shocker to a surprising number of people in golf tournament circles: The longer and bigger a course becomes, the longer it takes to get around. Holy Batman. Who could have seen that coming?

Besides an increase in cost to create and maintain, a course of bloated scale means less time with your playing partners as you zoom off tees, probably in carts, to find balls strewn across the landscape. The creature comforts of golf carts can disguise bloat when you have a loaded cooler, GPS and music playing (if that's your thing). But wheeling around a walkable course just isn't the same as the connection enjoyed on more proportionately

LENGTH of HOLE
1 MILE 273 YRDS
PAR — 3

The steadily increasing length derived from the continued improvements in the modern golf ball has already caused dismay to the designers of golf links, but when this length is enormously augmented by the baked state of the ground in a hot summer drastic reform in links architecture will be imperative. We venture a peep into the near future.

First Player : "Did you hit yours well, old chap ?"
Second Ditto : "Not very. I cut it a bit; but I think it's on the green !"

Long before they were invented, a circa 1925 cartoonist anticipated the need for carts as courses grew in distance to accommodate technological advances. (*Golf Illustrated*)

scaled grounds. And without getting too misty eyed and preachy, there is a metaphysical difference at day's end after strolling around a gently rolling, lovingly maintained golf course over driving an overbuilt mess requiring a cart.

WALKABILITY

> *The dog has seldom been successful in pulling man up to its level of sagacity, but man has frequently dragged the dog down to his.*
>
> JAMES THURBER

When things turned extra silly during the late 1980s and early 1990s golf course real-estate development boom, *Golf Digest* added a "walkability" score in a not-so-subtle reminder to raters that excessive mountain climbing was not to be rewarded. The advent of huge earthmoving equipment convinced developers to build on the least hospitable terrain, taking golf to mountainsides, lava beds and desertscapes unfriendly to people and canines. That's also when motorized carts became a significant and locked-in revenue source.

What could go wrong? A lot. As in hundreds of regrettable places unworthy of a Yes vote for Every Day fun.

Carts introduced many of us to golf as kids. The prospect of taking the wheel brightened an otherwise boring day tagging along with parents. Also, Club Cars and E-Z-GOs have allowed adaptive and older golfers to stay with the bloated scale of modern golf. And then there are the glorious holiday cart parades at The Villages that should never be discounted for their entertaining qualities. Cart revenue has even helped convince red-blooded capitalists to invest in improving maintenance while adding to the top line. Of course, carts do immense damage to turf. I believe that's what they call a wash.

However, there is an intangible quality to walking fairways you know were shaped by something other than a bulldozer. The golfer discovers a level of peace and calm breaking free of mechanized intrusions. Don't worry, I'm not about to insist from my cabin in the woods that golf was destroyed by buggies. But the freedom carts gave architects and developers to break from walkability ended up creating too many unlovable and unplayable courses no dog would enjoy.

Thankfully, the "minimalism" trend of the early 2000s returned to more walking-friendly designs unfettered by everything that came with carts and real estate-driven golf. In *Golfweek*'s ranking, the editors even introduced a "walk in the park" category for panelists to assess whether a course passed a basic test of scale and leisureliness. Ultimately, as with the dog friendliness question, there is more to this than walkability. We expect a golf stroll to look and feel good underfoot.

THE UNDERFOOT TEST

The site of a golf course should be there, not brought there.

PERRY MAXWELL, golf architect

Courses shifting toward natural design sensibilities have been shown to be more popular than those fighting the land. This has been proven by using available metrics such as rounds played, the price to play or join, maintenance budgets or the debt incurred by artificial designs needing to "fix" unpopular elements. Golfers of the 21st century are again tolerating and even coming to enjoy an unusual number of strange design elements interfering with their straight, easy path to the hole if the features *seem like they've always been there.*

But find a weird stance because the architect found a natural swale and merely converted it to turf?

That's my problem to overcome. I can handle this.

If land is shaped to pester or was rearranged for functional reasons and lacks a certain charm? One that does not feel right underfoot? We reject it.

Who put this nonsense here?

The best architects over time have taken this sense of immersion into nature so seriously that they will even carry the philosophy into daily play via a lack of signage, paved paths, visible irrigation boxes, bulbous tee markers and any number of things that distract from the very immersive sensibility they had hoped to create. Golfers have embraced this departure when given the chance, traveling absurd routes just to experience golf in the wild. Just ask anyone who has traveled to remote places like Bandon, Dornoch, Sand Hills or Barnbougle to encounter a special nature-driven disconnect. Most come back viewing golf and architecture in a new light.

Regardless of locale and course aesthetics, a key difference between man-made and natural often comes down to how drainage is handled. And now I know you're asking, do Normal People really need to think about the outflow of water when analyzing course design? Let me try.

The author's earliest days playing golf, no doubt more captivated by getting to be in a golf cart. Even one-wheeled versions without a roof. (Lynn Shackelford)

Drainage, drainage, drainage.

DONALD ROSS, golf architect

Holes are either found or brought to a site. A porous sandy base is ideal for growing turf and making the ball roll. Sometimes it is trucked in at great expense just so grown men playing for $20 million can play golf in white pants after a thunderstorm. If the soil is largely clay based, architects must design for drainage to get the grass to grow. Some designers will work hard to preserve existing natural drainage systems created by the preceding

A drain cap marked as "Ground Under Repair" just in case. (Geoff Shackelford)

architect: Mother Nature. Others move the land around and force water to go where they want it to go. The difference often changes how you perceive a design. Tees you might assume are dead-flat were most likely constructed with at least one percent tilt for those especially wet days, while surface drainage on the fairways is either preserved if already there, or it is created via a network of swales and slopes to move excess rainwater out of play and make growing grass easier. Done well, this artful shaping creates a less jarring "walk in the park" interrupted by muddy conditions, ugly drains or clunky landforms.

So why do so many modern designs feature oddly placed bowls with a drain cap at the bottom, only to be surrounded by a swarm of muddy divot scars? And always so close to play?

Not one, but three catch basins in a matter of yards really spoil the ground game around this green. (Geoff Shackelford)

Sometimes water absolutely must be promptly captured to prevent less savory run-off from reaching sensitive waterways that supply drinking water or that serve as home to fragile wildlife. Other times, the land is so dead flat for golf that the architect creates a collecting bowl, digs a hole at the center, fills it with gravel and then sticks a drain cap on top. These catch basins usually announce a rush job by the architect who lazily declared, *just send the water down below and move on!*

The installation of these drainage systems can be lucrative if your design fee takes ten percent of the construction budget, a common way architects charge the client of a new course. And some architects merely do not care about merging their design with the landscape in a seamless way, nor do they understand that most golfers loathe hitting off tightly mown lies at the base. Especially next to the green. Remember this when you barely miss a green and are in one of those basins that could just as easily have been placed a little farther from play.

The revered designers of the early 20th century had fewer construction tools. Sometimes, this forced them to leave well enough alone or cleverly merge drainage into the design. They were also not under as much pressure to cut the opening day ribbon. They learned from their predecessors and the ancient links that land unspoiled by a designer would be embraced no matter how quirky. The true artists of yesteryear took drainage seriously, ingeniously masking this vital bit of function via a system of tactfully graded slopes, swales, bumps, and other ground movement. When extreme weather came along, the rainfall would be sent away from the main playing areas and into a clever series of waterways and ditches. The only classic courses with basins and French drains were brought there by lesser talents.

There is even a noticeable difference in putting surface design due to drainage needs. The older the course, the more likely that greens will feel like mere extensions of the fairway and are only differentiated with a different mowing height. The newer the course, the more likely it has a complex subsurface drainage system commonly called a "USGA green." These systems have led to better putting conditions but are cumbersome to build and often feel divorced from the golf surrounding them. Any pronounced contours suddenly feel forced instead of like the ground leading into the green. To achieve a gentle melding with the fairway requires care that many courses built hurriedly tend to lack. When the greens get firmer and we try to land a ball short, the artificiality of a poorly done USGA green can be deflating when it rejects good shots. We're immediately reminded that someone not named Mother Nature is jacking with our score.

QUIET BEAUTY

When I speak of a hole being inspiring, it is not intended to infer that the visitor is to be subject to attacks of hysteria on every teeing ground as he casts his eye over the fairway to the green for the first time, and to be so overwhelmed with the outstanding features, both natural and manufactured, that he cannot keep his eye on the ball.

                                                A.W. TILLINGHAST

Some golfers cannot be talked out of loving a manicured landscape dotted with ornamental flower beds, bright white bunkers, pruned trees and ornamental fairway striping. Others love the unpredictability of a natural dunescape with a softer color palette. And many more desire something in between: a controlled setting that feels just authentic enough without becoming lost ball nightmare.

I'm not going to try to dissuade from adoring the artificial introduction of color such as bright-red cedar mulch, or flowers and flowering trees or shrubbery, unless the faux add-ons spell out the course's name. Such garish displays are only useful as a place for your dog to do as he pleases. Nor can I convince all golfers that fake waterfalls, fountains spurting out of artificial, rock-lined lakes, miles of stone walls and cart path curbs that could stop a big rig needlessly spoil the land and weigh down the green fee. Have it your way. If you find these environments pleasing enough for a stroll with Baxter and don't mind the extra cost, then it's a place you'd enjoy spending four or so hours around. We all have our own aesthetics.

Besides, there is always some form of beauty to be found on 99.9 percent of golf courses. Maybe it's that one mature oak still standing at the 15th tee after six hurricanes and how the place looks in the fall. Or it's

The quiet beauty of a par-4 from the tee. But wild fairway contours awaiting the tee shot at Santa Anita's par-4 18th, only add to its charm. (Geoff Shackelford)

those mountain views on the back nine offering a peaceful perspective found nowhere else. Perhaps it's a satisfying combination of fresh air, quiet, singing birds and turf, similar to those idyllic downstream pools where fly fishermen love to cast their dry flies—even if the brook trout aren't rising.

For evaluating whether a course meets this grand composition of scale, walkability, naturalness and beauty, ask if you could leave your clubs in the trunk, take Toto for a walk and savor the stroll? If the answer is yes, then the course checks off some or all the aforementioned architectural boxes. And if the place lets you bring your dog along for a round? Bonus points!

Chapter 6

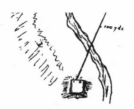

TESTING R-E-D: CONFLICT AVOIDANCE, THE RANKINGS, R-E-D NUMBERS, MATCH PLAY(ING) AND BUCKET LISTING

*Other fun ways to enjoy golf architecture
without losing your mind*

*Criticizing a golf course is like going into a man's family. The fond
mother trots up her children for admiration. Only a boor would
express anything else than high opinion. So it is a thankless task to
criticize a friend's home golf course. 'Where ignorance is bliss 'tis folly
to be wise.' It is natural one should love his home course. He knows
it, and with golf holes familiarity does not breed contempt, but quite
the reverse.*

C.B. MACDONALD, golf architect

You've hopefully taken the big three questions out for a test drive before we make the turn and head for the finishing holes. If not, then permission granted! Those who've jumped ahead are undoubtedly basking in the joys of increased awareness pondering a design's rememberability, pleasurability and (dog) walkability. An eye for quality over junk has developed. Tastes have been refined. Under-appreciated courses are now cherished even if they are unranked. You finally put a finger on what you dislike about a slog of a design, but could never pinpoint this to your golf pals, who always insist on booking a tee time there.

Perhaps you even developed new theories about design intent. It now makes sense why the architect put those bunkers on the 4th hole tee shot: to reward a smart and well-executed shot that averts them. Or the seemingly boring hole that you once insisted needed help has, on further reflection, subtle features that suddenly make sense when the hole is cut in certain locations. And that seemingly boring stretch of holes on the back nine you never understood? They turned out to be an understated change-of-pace attempt, complete with subdued-but-sticky features meant to give golfers a wee break before the tough finishing holes.

This more developed critical eye comes with increased awareness and mild risk factors, which, if not kept in check, could lead to a Normalcy deficiency. Armed with the three big and seemingly harmless key questions to ask of a design, conclusions confidently shared out loud can easily rub some the wrong way. Consequently, the primary goal of this chapter is to help you maintain friendships, retain access to fun places, and avoid a trip to the ER after your critique is answered with a sucker punch because you insulted someone's home course.

So let's ease in to the messy game of evaluating designs with two suggestions only to be broken out when faced with an onslaught of absurd claims.

In speaking of courses, each man believes that his own is far and away better than most others...he brings to mind the niblick shot he played he played in such and such a match; where else could that have been done? He saw Hagen take a 78 on a course, and no one can prove to him that they have a better layout at so and so.

GEORGE THOMAS, golf architect

A course-ranking panelist was raving to me about a new course that landed on the *Golf Digest* Top-100 list in its first year of eligibility. I was skeptical of the design merits knowing how the architect was prone to take on sites only a Siberian husky could traverse. The buzzy architect du jour had delivered another club-of-the-moment only accessible to twenty players a day but beloved by single-digit handicappers who could brag to their golf buddies how: (A) they managed to get on the place when others had no chance, and (B) the new masterpiece busted their chops and therefore must be a winner! This big, bold and new vino in town reportedly has notes of tangerine and Zasavica goat cheese. But on multiple tastings, it turns out to be a $4-dollar plonk with a $100 story.

As I listened to the praise for this modern masterpiece, the panelist put on the full-court press, convinced I wanted to be sold on its merits. He mentioned the "good routing" for a tough mountainside site. You can imagine how much that resonated.

Waiter, bring me a double anything!

The panelist then noted the "perfect blend of yardages" and other stuff about shot values he had to check off for the balloting system. Finally, after again hearing how tough-but-fair this tour de force played for a single digit like him, I'd hear enough.

"So would you want to play there every day?"

The panelist winced. "Oh, hell, no!"

"What about ever again?"

"Na." And he laughed. Perhaps my return volleys had been delivered deftly enough?

From there the conversation drifted into other topics after it was apparent I had not been sold on the course's big first impression, testing qualities or ability to check off all the ranking boxes. Shocker of all shockers, the course debuted high in the Top 100 only to crater and fall off the list within ten years when sensibilities finally changed. Even good players grew tired of the torture, and enough panelists threw up their hands and refused to reward the misery over the joys delivered by hundreds of other designs.

Here's another creative way to make a point without starting a brawl: Try a subtle memorability pop quiz. Maybe after hearing a bunch of nonsense you don't agree with, or even more malarky about a design you know isn't your cup of tea, you can probe the issue politely, patiently. Perhaps someone is droning on about how they rake his or her bunkers three times a day and sends out a forecaddie with every group to look for lost balls because no one has broken 70 there yet. Then cut 'em off and try this: Randomly suggest that you heard about the fascinating 7th hole.

If the other party begins scratching his head and the dandruff flakes fly as he tries to recall the 7th, you've got your opening. In the gentlest of tones you can explain how the design may not be living up to the hype if the hole is so forgettable. But—BUT—if this is his new home course, avoid the wise-guy follow-up. Let the question stand and move on to talking about the weather. No need to move in for the kill and highlight how the 7th remains a wildly forgettable passageway from the 6th green to the 8th tee.

Now, let's get to the delicate businesses of rankings, scoring, quibbling, course match play and other forms of golf architecture debate.

R-E-D VS. THE RANKINGS

The reason for the survival of the awards system is purely commercial.
ROBERT HENRI

To be clear, I have empathy for those attempting to rank golf courses within often incongruous parameters and overseen by meddling editors. Full confession: I'm a recovering panelist who saw the inner workings of this racket while contributing to various publications. So you may catch whiffs of cynicism in what I'm about to share with you about the rankings.

A thoroughly late 20th-century creation, the Top 100 lists by magazine panels have improved awareness of a course design's role in your life and at times sparked a pursuit of creating golf courses with more permanent qualities. If you opened this book hoping to become a more complete, confident and satisfied golf connoisseur after questioning one of the rankings, a hearty thank you to the lists of the world.

Awards and rankings continue to facilitate the restoration of run-down and mangled classics and have brought respect and notoriety to under-appreciated gems designed by once-overlooked architects. There is also a trend toward more lists centered around fun, pure design quality and affordability. We're hopefully saying goodbye to exclusive shows of excess that later prove light on substance. Nevertheless, the lists still have a ways to go before shaking their well-earned reputations as elitist water-cooler gatherings rife with conflicts and occasional corruption.

The unending appeal of rankings, awards and lists means they are not going away even if the magazines that publish them fold. Lists make us think. They punch buttons. They give us fun stuff to discuss after a round. They inflate and deflate egos. They've even been known to reward outstanding work and fuel positive neighborhood competitions, sometimes leading to better end-products for golfers. But they also can be conflict-ridden contradictions. In this mixed-bag manner, golf course rankings are hardly different than any other awards-based efforts to recognize hotels, movies, wines and songs. They can seem unfair or compromised. And indeed, sometimes they are.

While researching this book, I went back to bookmarked links of old rankings from just a few years prior and nearly all of them redirected me to the latest ranking of whatever it was, a sad admission that access to old lists might remind us how many courses of fleeting fancy were rewarded only to be discarded.

Still, the most noble lists do their best to reward the pinnacle of the profession in question. They encourage aspirational thinking from those whose job it is to imagine how to put new twists on classic ideas. Some award-worthy artistes are motivated by the quest for notoriety. They work harder, fueled by dreams of donning a tux and indulging us with a teary thank you speech until an orchestra announces their forty-five seconds are up. Most golfers know by now that course rankings and "Best Of" awards sometimes deliver perspective, occasionally reward grand efforts and, most of all, generate revenue for the people who publish the lists.

As of this writing, it costs *Golf Digest*'s 2,000 or so panelists $300 a year for the privilege of "rating" courses, and new members pay a hefty initiation fee. *Golfweek*'s panel must attend for-profit "educational" outings quite often at courses eager to be noticed. And just like that, the aspirational benefits of the awards system gets crushed 9&8 by commercial incentive. It must also be noted that golf somehow survived, grew and produced legions of stellar designs for two centuries—at least—before any ranking was ever published. These exercises, therefore, do not "grow the game."

There is little use in examining the absurdities produced by rankings or to revisit a recent scandal causing an overhaul of one prominent list, complete with an American huckster sporting a fake British accent, free first-class plane tickets, "fired" panelists and other shenanigans all to get a virtual polo field near Bangkok into the World Top 100. Plus, challenging unscrupulous, diva-like panelists would unfairly discount the earnest efforts of the vast majority who follow the guidelines set out for them, take their work seriously and agonize over how to grade a course.

For our purposes, it's vital to remember that the modern introduction of rankings started from a terrible place—the 200 toughest courses—and sadly maintained its penchant for par protection well past the sell-by date. This was *Golf Digest*'s "Resistance to Scoring," arguably the worst thing to ever happen to golf architecture over its fifty-year reign of terror. It was about as logical as rewarding films for how long they take to end.

Since ranking panelists rarely pay green fees and are typically only required to play a course one time to vote, the factors delivering consistent fun can be overlooked. "Raters" are not required to walk the course free of their clubs to see more, and maybe learn of local nuances or prevent score bias. After just one round, panelists must give scores for categories rewarding difficulty and other mysterious stuff like "Shot Values." Plenty of voters have rewarded a course's resistance to scoring because of what they shot, another reason Resistance to Scoring should have long ago been rebranded Resistance to Fun. Thankfully, it's been retired.

Some rankings started as grouping of ten (11–20, etc.) and others have contemplated simpler questions or general "star" designations to not cost superintendents their jobs all because a place falls from 23rd to 25th after a slight dip in the Conditioning score. But we humans love our numbered rankings and want to know down to the decimal point where the place finished on the list. The lists have nobly tried to make a just system out of what is inevitably a subjective pursuit, no matter how hard the "editors" try

Cypress Point screams beauty and ambiance even when the holes are not playing along the Pacific Ocean. (Geoff Shackelford)

to remove biases from the process. But they still engineer outcomes, which even means poring over panel scorecards in search of outliers that can be tossed. This policing can get ugly, at least based on the number of annoyed panelists eager to tell their stories to ranking skeptics like yours truly.

I'm no statistician, but you'd think having a force of 2,000 would allow for them to drop out the highest and lowest scores, tally the numbers up and be done with it. Instead, the obsessing over extreme scores in categories can lead to terse phone calls from mysterious number crunchers suggesting that some raters had submitted too many outlying numbers. My all-time favorite story came from a panelist regarding the score he assigned to Cypress Point for its atmospherics.

Even on the foggiest, dankest day, Alister MacKenzie's masterpiece takes the golfer on a glorious excursion through Monterey Pines and

Cypress, then over stunning white sand dunes, all before finishing with a legendary stretch atop a weathered cliff—all while sea lions bark, otters play and golfers swear they've left earth for some celestial place. The panelist gave Cypress Point a 10 for "Ambience," apparently too far north of the mean. He was ordered to reassess. Sternly. Naturally, he was flummoxed. His role as a voter seemed at risk for assessing that the "feel and atmosphere" Cypress Point was, well, a 10. And if this place is not the ultimate in that department, then nothing in golf is even an 8. So why have a scale of 1 to 10 in the first place? Or panelists at all?

And then there are the murkier matters raters must deal with at certain publications, ranging from virtual indoctrination seminars, terse instructions to visit certain courses or, wink-wink, required rounds at places that want to be rated—almost always a red flag! And these noble warriors of evaluation face relentless consequences for non-herd-like behavior, constantly on edge, trying to manage multiple ancillary factors instead of focusing on the stuff that matters. This is all before the chaos that takes place when the votes are tabulated and other "factors" are woven into the final listing. Also known as, whatever goes on behind closed doors in the name of pleasing advertisers and friends of the brand.

The ranking mishegoss has not cost lives or made the planet warmer. But the ridiculousness did inspire offering up a simpler way of evaluating courses.

R for Remember ever hole after you play.

E for Every Day playability and interest.

D for Dog walking friendliness (and friendliness to dogs).

Each of these questions speaks to golf architecture's most important micro-topics. And unlike some of the more elaborate rankings, these Normal questions are intentionally simple. I recommend keeping it that way. But if

you want to go above and beyond to pinpoint the very best courses, I naturally have suggestions!

R-E-D NUMBERS

The only real solid numbers involved are in the rankings themselves.
                    DESMOND MUIRHEAD, golf architect

A simple score is a common go-to for golf course discussions. I'm a fan of
old -fashioned 1-to-10 scales. They give plenty of leeway if you're building
a personal list of favorite places or want to compare courses. Architect
Tom Doak used 1-to-10 for his *Confidential Guide to Golf Courses*, another
important 1990s contribution to the widening discourse on golf architecture. His system is commonly referred to as the Doak Scale, sometimes
nauseatingly so by architectural loonies eager to flash insider credentials.
But we love them, anyway.

Golf Digest and *Golfweek* also use 1-to-10 scores for categories, while
Golf magazine uses a bucket scoring system to place courses where their
panel places a design within the top 250 or so courses. A 1-to-5 scoring
system is strangely prohibitive given the vast array of courses (and in some
cases, an apparent sin of ascribing a 10). But any of these options are worth
considering if you decide to drill a bit deeper with R-E-D. You might want
to settle a score between courses you love after all three check off the R, E,
and D questions with a resounding yes. Or maybe you'd like to work out if
you prefer Bethpage Black or Red. Or maybe your inner design geek thinks
the Red quietly is better because it's more varied, possesses more memorable
characteristics, and is more walkable—all nudging it further into Every Day
friendly territory than the Black. Most, I believe, would find the Black's
18 holes way more memorable—and, perhaps, most of those memories are

vivid only because of the sheer fear, dread and incredulity they invoke. In any case, you are the judge. Assign a score to each of the three categories, add up the score, and settle the differences.

I would begin to grow concerned about your life priorities and mental health if you were to assign scores to each of the main areas of the R-E-D system. Drilling down that deeply is unnecessarily excessive, and, well, not exactly how normal people should lead their lives. A "Yes" or "No" should work most of the time. But, if you are still at odds with a golf buddy over design merits, there is another method worth considering.

MATCH PLAY(ING) COURSES

Match play, you see, is much more of a joust. It calls for a doughty, resourceful competitor, the sort of fellow who is not ruffled by his opponent's fireworks and is able to set off a few of his own when it counts.

HERBERT WARREN WIND, golf writer

Debates over favorite courses tend to get chippy when pitting one course against another—particularly if any of the disputants holds even a slightest stake in either venue. These should be fun and fruitful debates, but they can also expose unconscious biases about how the place makes you *feel*, which tends to color judgment.

That lovable gasbag Cliff Clavin of "Cheers" fame might dare to say it's the quality mixology making his beloved watering hole superior, but we're also aware, because of the bar tagline, that this is a place where everyone knows your name. Which is certainly part of its charm. But if we made Cliff play a match against another pub, with categories applicable to the refined art of comparing libation-serving establishments, we might expose a few holes in his biases. And that's where the simplicity of golf architecture match play comes in handy.

This tool for preventing knockdown, drag-out golf architectural bickering was taught to me by the Morrissett Brothers, purveyors of the Golf Club Atlas website that's been another key driver of golf architecture's 21st-century spike in connoisseurship. The site's reviews and discussion have made it more acceptable to indulge in refining one's design sensibilities while shifting the conversation away from superficial qualities to those built around fun.

The brothers employed match play after agreeing that, while many courses were fantastic, it was tricky to judge which one was better. It is perfectly normal for golfers to want to compare designs in a similar neighborhood or, perhaps, when two places land in similar spots on a list. The urge to compare layouts is often the first discussion topic you hear unsolicited when golfers return from multi-course complexes or golf-saturated regions. Instead of naming a favorite layout, we often resort to just comparing it to the others.

"Bandon Trails was great, but it's no Pacific Dunes," is a typical assessment you might hear from someone lucky enough to play the two.

That's all fine and dandy. However, was this conclusion reached because you loved the ocean views? Or did you find more holes to your liking at one course over the other? Unless this kind of First World comparison shopping foments into a dispute over course conditioning or how the course "made you feel," such banter does add to the joy of examining, post-round, why a great design is, indeed, great. And let's face it: This totally beats the agony of being on the receiving end of someone's shot-by-shot, hole-by-hole, post-game analysis of their round.

And then on 15, I necked a drive but it worked out and my rangefinder said 156 but there as a helping wind and….

Please, no!

But blow-by-blow, knockdown-dragout match play?

Much more fun and far less tedious.

Facing off two designs works best with an opponent sharing some-what similar tastes, values and wisdom. Here's the recipe. It might be called "Golf Course Grilling"

SERVES 2

Grilling time: *5 minutes, maximum*

Ingredients: *Select two golf course designs of roughly similar overall design merits*

Scorecards for both courses (usually easily acquired online)

Best paired with a cold pint in warm weather

or an Irish coffee on a nippy day

- Start at the first hole. Ask which has the stronger opening hole? The first at Ye Olde Majestic Creek is a wide-open par-5 meant to get players away. The starting hole at Gator Creek National is a mid-length par-4 that plays to the base of a still smoldering volcano and is a thriller. They do not seem at all comparable design-wise. Let this go. We have 18 to work with here.

- You both agree that Gator's opener is a neat par-4 and agree to give it the win even though Ye Olde's opener was under-designed to ease golfers into a round where an epic finishing stretch awaits along Raymond's Creek.

- If Ye Olde Majestic is a more complete design sporting many supe-rior holes, it can eventually prevail over 18.

- Do not stop to argue about the incongruity of comparisons between wildly different holes. Tell them to lighten up. Call it a tie. Halves are fine. Excuse me, ties as they are now called in the Rules of Golf after a 200-year run.

- Take a sip and move to the next hole.
- Absolutely keep a running score to the last hole. Some courses peak early and might close out the match. Frequent refrains might go something like, "Doonesbury Creek closed it out on the 13th tee over Peanuts National!" Do not take off your caps and shake hands. Keep going. That 7&6 win by Doonesbury Creek might end up much closer due to Peanuts's epic finishing stretch, thus turning the match into a mere 1-up affair.
- Take another sip and toast to a hard-fought battle.

EVERY DAY, BUCKET LIST STYLE

If I had to be sentenced to play only one course the rest of my life, I would pick St Andrews in Scotland, because it changes so much, and there's nothing about it that's obvious.

BOBBY JONES on The Old Course

You've won the Mega Millions. You've suddenly come from regal bloodlines and are attaching suffixes to your name. No more covers to protect your expensive new irons. You can join any exclusive place in the world and fly private to the course of your dreams, where they will know your name. The tee is open whenever you're ready. Inevitably, you'll pick the place of your grandest dreams. Quite often golfers will share the name of such a course unsolicited, proving we golfers are a dream-prone bunch. And, quite often, a respondent might name a course he or she had just played, with excitement still fresh. Or, it could be a course that's named for bragging rights, usually

Tiger Woods and Jack Nicklaus pose on the Swilcan burn bridge at the 2022 Open Championship. Both men have said they love playing the Old Course more than any other in the world. (Geoff Shackelford)

an exclusive private club that's nearly impossible to get on. But those are easy to smoke out by asking R-E-D questions.

Plenty of others have never contemplated the one-and-only question. How sad! Get out and buy some lottery tickets and dream, dammit!

If you had just one course to play every day until you check out of Hotel Earth, which on would it be?

The answer to your Heavenly, Only One Course Every Day question: Is the place so supremely above average that you know after just one round that you could play it in perpetuity? Courses in this category obviously get the passing grade under the Every Day parameters, but "the one" is your otherworldly, First Team, All-World dreamboat melding beauty, good vibes, thrilling shots and a collection of holes that leave you dreaming about more rounds there.

A great icebreaker at a golf event is asking golfers to share their reasons for choosing the one course they would play if the Golf Gods granted such a gift. Forced to select just one, we throw vanity and other arbitrary values out the window and focus on the place that affected us the way no other course has.

Mine is North Berwick, but it was a grueling extra holes showdown with the Old Course at St Andrews and Cypress Point. Cruden Bay and Royal Dornoch are close behind. Yes, I've been blessed.

A final note: Bobby Jones, Jack Nicklaus and Tiger Woods all named, unsolicited, the Old Course as their "one and only." The town, the people and the fond memories of career highlights certainly played a role. But all three picked The Old because of what its design brought out in them as master strategists and legendary practitioners. It's wild to realize that the very first course with enduring soul remains the ultimate bucket list destination for golf's GOATs.

Chapter 7

EASY WAYS TO OUTSMART THE DESIGN: READING THE ARCHITECT'S MIND AND SCORING BETTER

*Aerial recon, studying local knowledge
and other ways to improve*

*When he has taught himself to study a hole from the point of view
of the man who laid it out, he will be much more likely to play it
correctly.*

BOBBY JONES

Twenty years ago, I wrote *Grounds for Golf*, a course design primer. Nearly all of the ideas put forward in this chapter could not even be pondered for that book. Meaning, the delicate matter of researching and picking apart architecture is constantly in flux due to technology, the availability of information and what the Rules of Golf allow. For all the life-changing advice this chapter imparts based on my years of observing, playing and designing, evidence suggests that blissful ignorance transcends the generations and will always play an underrated role in playing world-class golf.

However, if the suggestions presented here are used judiciously, you should be able to weed out architectural noise, overcome deceptive touches, make more rational decisions from the tee and employ your heightened architectonic senses to deftly attack a well-designed hole. Shot execution is still very much up to you. But discovering local secrets can be satisfying architectural detective work that many golfers resist as if a course is supposed to have no secrets. Advantage, you, dear reader.

ALMOST NOTHING THE PROS DO APPLIES TO YOU... ALMOST

The hazards and bumps on the course are there to offer a challenge to the skill, courage and philosophy of the player, who suffers no interference in his game except from nature. The geography of the course, the temper of the elements, the quality of his courage and the unevenness of his temperament are the obstacles to be overcome.

ROBERT HARRIS, golf official and writer

Professional golfers are the world's most curious flock. Most care little about architecture despite a job description demanding they master golf courses. The world's last rugged individualists—who wear anklet socks and own fifty pairs of white slacks—function as a herd in ways both peculiar and adorable.

Jordan Spieth and caddie Michael Greller ponder a shot at Southern Hills during the 2022 PGA Championship. (Geoff Shackelford)

Take their lingo. They'll say "reps" instead of "practice." "Physio" instead of "masseur." "Rinsed" instead of "I hit the ball in the %$#@*!# water." Some of this linguistic code signals they're inside the ropes and in a cool kids' club. But anthropologists would interpret this peculiar language as grooming for other aberrant behaviors they will later assume as full-fledged members of the elite social stratum known as professional golf.

For instance, not walking in a "through-line" of a peer's next putt while going to tap in yours, was a big thing for many years. This seemed like a nice show of courtesy until some superstitious minds saw the gesture to passive-aggressively say: "Since you're going to miss that putt, I don't want to step in your next line."

Now that everyone can tap down spike marks, tiptoeing around through-lines is less of a big deal.

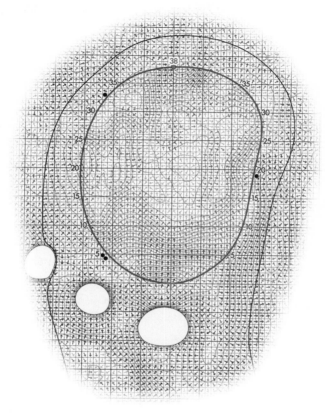

The green reading chart used by players for a time to read putts. (Strokesaver)

Normal players have always mimicked the behaviors and playing styles—and even parroted the opinions—of the pros. This certainly extends to course design. For example, in his power-of-positive-thinking-mode, Gary Player declared every course he was playing the best of its kind, which seemed disingenuous. Other pros also avoided publicly critiquing course design, possibly out of false flattery for the course, or possibly because they lacked any real insight to share. Tiger Woods has been known to mention how he approves of a course because "it's all right in front of you," an underwhelming, even vacuous observation to those who value some mystery in their golf architecture. It could be deflating to hear the one player capable of tackling the more intricate designs also give such a banal description. Particularly since Woods could pick up on the smallest details, discover the seemingly undiscoverable, then go to bed visualizing targets and shots no other player would dare. Perhaps it was a ruse? A strategy to lull the rest of the field into assuming that there really isn't much to think about? If Tiger says it's 'all in front of you,' then why, they might figure, should they waste time deconstructing a course's design as part of a game plan?

Green reading books with alarming heat maps and hundreds of tiny arrows became a thing after a few players believed they putted better using them. Tournaments were pressured into releasing hole locations the night prior so players and caddies could pencil the pin placement into their book, get out their protractors, and prepare for the next day's round. Players could even visualize breaks they might face, or put the information under their pillows for sweet dreams. And it was all a bit too mechanical, stripping the game of another skill. Solving breaks and other putting subtleties under enormous pressure was something fans appreciated.

Even the greatest feel putters jumped on the green reading book madness. They followed the herd no matter how little sense it made. I chuckled watching two of the greatest to ever roll a ball on closely cropped turf—Tiger Woods and Jordan Spieth—squat down like catchers and sheepishly peak at the green book between their thighs, as if they were trying to hide a pitch sign from a prying third base coach. These two have accomplished otherworldly things by trusting hand-eye coordination and photographic memories of past putts. They both demonstrate pure genius on the greens as have only few others. Yet they bought in for a while. Spieth even admitted his two greatest putting weeks were on courses where green books were banned or unavailable (Augusta National and the Old Course), yet he still leaned on this crutch, as most others did from 2014 to 2021. Rule changes then returned good old-fashioned eyeballing after the USGA and R&A recognized green reading as a vital, time-honored skill. Players went back to reading putts with their eyes or the occasional line straddling. The world's best were still broke par. The sun continued to rise from the east.

Another fad they've moved on is still wildly relevant for the rest of us: employing Google Earth to scout a course. For those of you with good internet, I bring tips!

AERIAL RECON

Take the bird's eye view of the situation before choosing to react. A change in position can change everything.

ARIELLE FORD, writer

As Google started building its vast online aerial photography archive during the early 2000s, good golfers would casually mention in press conferences how they had given the course a once-over from above. Good college players and budding pros who had yet to build an analytics team would say that what little they knew of a tournament course came from poking around online. I'd ask what they saw in this aerial recon.

Some resisted revealing their secrets. Most could not pin down exactly what they learned from the 30,000-foot perspective other than it helped them. Ultimately, it became clear they were not gleaning the details you'd expect. Instead, they were trying to answer "lay of the land" questions. Stuff like…

- Where is the range and what kind of short game practice can I do?
- Is the 10th tee close to the clubhouse and what kind of tee shot is it (in case I start there)?
- How many holes have water?
- What street do I turn on to reach the parking lot?
- Is there a Starbucks nearby and a Chipotle on the way home?

Answers to such questions saved pros time. They previously followed the herd approach of playing a big-time tournament venue months or weeks prior. But, after a few of these trips, sojourning players realized the courses weren't at peak tournament conditions, providing their sneak peek no real advantage. Or they grew weary of club members asking pesky stuff like: "Who's the nicest guy on Tour?"

During this time, stats, yardage and green mapping books became more precise, ushering in a "let my team do the pre-research" era. This allowed pros to rest up physically and mentally leading up to a tournament. This less-is-more approach also let players focus on "lines" pre-selected by the team. I will not discourage you from thinking this sounds like extreme handholding. After all, aerial image reconnaissance provides a useful tool for the rest of us.

Answering simple logistical questions reduces uncertainty in a relentlessly unpredictable sport. When it's an extra special course where you want to savor the experience and avoid the worry over feeling out of your element, getting a "lay of the land" can allay some of the anxiety that comes with the famous places. Aerial analysis can also help if you're playing a business round and want to reduce the chance of doing something fatally wrong (or just want to make sure you arrive on time!).

Whether you use Google Maps on a mobile phone or download the free Google Earth to your desktop for increased functionality and historic image access, there is little harm in taking a bird's eye tour. By opening up these incredible images, clicking on the lower left "layers," and poking around to see how the holes are sequenced, you can answer questions that otherwise might be time-wasters of your host or the pro shop. Just promise me this: If you do go somewhere for the first time, let the host be a host. Play dumb. Don't admit to your scouting effort. They'll like you more if they get to be your guide. Do not finish their sentences. They pay good money for the privilege of welcoming you into their home.

OBSERVING BUT NOT OBSESSING

I thought about what my crows saw as they flew above canyons and treetops, the birds-eye view of life. They would recognize specific trees, perches, and nesting sites from a completely different perspective than I could. Their maps differed from mine; they knew the topography, the contours of the landscape, on a much grander scale.

ELIZABETH CHURCH, writer

After you find an online scorecard (super easy), the routing can be pieced together, and you should be able to make a sounder decision on which tees are best to play. Just keep in mind that, in an aerial image, the distance between back and forward tees can appear farther apart than they actually are.

As we peruse, the handwringer in all of us will immediately zoom in on optimal spots to miss a drive on the more nettlesome-looking holes. There is no shame in this type of planning, but remember that this exercise

The second shot at Pebble Beach's par-5 6th is blind from the landing area, but the Google Earth view of Pebble Beach's 6th allows for a pre-round recon study to see what awaits atop the hill. (Geoff Shackelford, Google Earth)

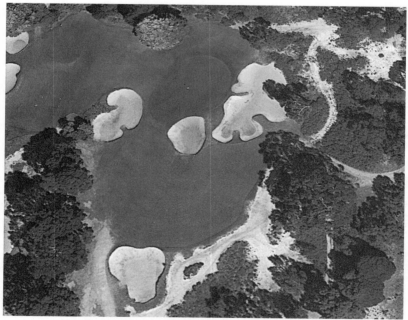

The par-3 7th at Victoria Golf Club in Australia plays slightly uphill and an infinity green effect presents a sense of mystery. But viewed from above in Google Earth, the front pin screams "sucker" and the aerial perspective shows plenty of safe space to play to past the pin. (Geoff Shackelford, Google Earth)

should be about lowering the stress level, not spiking it. Don't spend your pre-research obsessing over how each drop area plays when, not if, you "rinse" tee shots. That's a practice round no-no. Also, keep in mind that a two-dimensional satellite view can be limited, so avoid spending too much thought and deliberation on certain features. Here a few suggestions.

Do not dwell. For example, over forced carries. And do not place too much importance on obvious boundary lines that may not come into play, even on your worst shots. Know that they may not look nearly as imposing at ground level. Prone to shove-slicing tee shots? Don't spend a lot of time scrolling over to the Pacific Ocean when scouting out Pebble Beach's front nine. While your sports psychology team might view this as excessively negative, it's okay to take note of places to bail out or lay up. Think of it is as worst-case comprehensive planning.

Do not presume too much about the architectural quality. From a connoisseurship perspective, the 30,000-foot view puts the property parameters in perspective. You might get some idea what the course architect faced before the course was built by seeing what the surrounding area looks like. This can sometimes prove upsetting when you see gently rolling countryside interrupted by an overbuilt course full of fake hazards and mounds. Still, do not let this form of recon be your sole guide in judging design character. These images are generally taken in bright, midday light guaranteed to flatten out contours. I've seen too many courses look dull from the air only to be full of nuance, groovy ground features, beauty and character.

Do not obsess about scale. Tree-lined fairways will appear narrower than they really are, particularly if the image is taken when shadows cut into visible fairway acreage. Greens generally look tinier than they'll be when you play the course, and the trouble can look more menacing if you stare too long. Dive just deep for a quick dip, but not so long that you drown.

Do not take a nostalgic trip down memory lane. Thanks to a Google feature allowing for easy reference to past overheads, you can look at a course before and after changes were made. Or, see what the place looks like in winter versus summer. Just keep an eye on the clock.

DECIPHERING DECEPTION

> *You could make a pretty good living standing near any green at any country club or public course in America and betting even money that the next approach shot you saw would be short of hole high. Watch it the next time you play. Most golfers are consistently short of the pin, even short of the green…hardly ever does the average golfer go over the green.*

> ARNOLD PALMER

Rarely did pros cite hazard placement as a vital intel reveal during recon missions. Maybe they just kept certain secrets to themselves? Either way, studying the situation of various hazards can save strokes and answer key questions about the architect's intent.

Here comes the next big design reveal to make this book tax deductible: Architects rarely punish golfers for taking an extra club. The outcome of going long is rarely fatal. Maybe a slick downhill chip or delicate bunker shot awaits, but there are very few copies of the Road hole out there where all sorts of misery awaits a shot gone long. (Please do not send me photos of infinity greens where the world drops off behind. I'm aware of their existence.)

Yet most golfers leave shots short. Ego has been known to influence club selection. Really, it's true. Thankfully, dear reader, you have never tried to hood-muscle a 7-iron when only a stock 5-iron was called for, all in an apparent effort to demonstrate how well your new golf fitness regimen is working.

Of Earth's hundreds of thousands of golf holes, a vast majority feature the worst stuff in front. Bunkers are generally the architect's favorite tool for deceiving a golfer or to make a course look tougher. In trying to appease the opposing forces of playability and eye-candy, architects purposely place traps well short of the putting surface for visual excitement without making the target impossible to hit. They also do it off the tee.

Sometimes the point of placing a bunker only 130 yards from the tee is not to punish a hack, but rather to steer decent-strikers away from a liability issue, such as another tee or home near the property. Other times, they are tucked annoyingly near your sweet spot off the tee to deliver a reward for taking on the risk. Suddenly, you've discovered from aerial recon work which bunkers incentivize and which are just there to punish.

Even golfers who have played hundreds of rounds at a course with some deceptively placed bunkering still fall for a pit placed far from the green. It's been a thing in golf for hundreds of years, so don't beat yourself up. But, from above, you can now easily spot some of these design touches and take mental notes. Please do. Because when you're at ground level and come face to face with an artfully camouflaged situation, the gut reaction is to believe what you see before you, dismissing what the aerial revealed. The hole, at ground level was designed to include an optical illusion. Should you be having a pitiful day clouding your judgment, this advance prep work will deliver some much-needed calm and coherent analysis to your decision-making.

THOSE PESKY ANGLES

> *The whole secret lies in confusing the enemy, so that he cannot fathom our real intent.*
>
> SUN TZU, *The Art of War*

The bird's eye view highlights another grand design trick even the world's best fall prey to: the meaning of angles. A wide, perpendicular green will play the same yardage to a left or right hole location. But tilt the green placement just a bit and it can make one side play a club longer. Or more. At ground level, the magnitude of this difference is not always clear. Architects sometimes do this on purpose. In other cases, the arrangement of features leads to subtleties even the designer never imagined while laying out the course. This is sometimes the case with "sucker" pins, where the slightest angling of features means a safe shot to the middle of the green would have reduced your penchant for dramatic triple bogeys.

There is no more famous example of pesky angles than the 12th at Augusta National. Golfers of a certain vintage will never forget CBS announcer Ken Venturi's annual pleas during Masters broadcasts. I'm paraphrasing here, but his profound guidance usually went something like this: "Play to the center of the green and take your three!"

No matter how conspicuous the conundrum, some of golf's greatest still played at the far right hole location knowing the 14-yard distance difference between the front left and front right. The wind at Amen Corner has sent many shots into Rae's Creek where the trouble always arises from a steadfast and pressure-induced refusal to believe how much more club is needed to reach the far-right pins.

From the tee? It all looks so quaint and benevolent. The trees. The flowers. Glistening light bouncing off the flagstick. A short iron in hand. And all that perfect green grass around the cup. What's to lose except a free dinner every Tuesday evening of Masters week for the rest of their days?

Turns out, little good comes from playing at the flag. Ever.

How many times have you seen a player finish well long of the Sunday hole location at Augusta National? Pretty much never.

These images show Lost Farm at Barnbougle Dunes and the par-5th 8th. The ground view shows an intimidating bunker and steep pitch to the green from right to left. However, from above, the bunker turns out to be well short of the green and that steep pitch is not evident, making the fall off to the right look more intimidating than the ground view. This shows how aerial reconnaissance can be both valuable and very different once playing the course. (Geoff Shackelford, Google Earth)

NOTICING QUADRANTS

A putting green has features just like a human, or, at least, it should have to be worthy of the name.

A.W. TILLINGHAST, golf architect

In addition to those pesky angles, architects love to create "wings" whose size, shape and meaning can be tricky to discern from the fairway. The old architects loved bizarre green shapes and were not held back by the complications of constructing a USGA green, which features multiple subterranean layers that must all match to promote drainage and healthy turf. But because these greens require more precision than just shaping a nice pile of sand, we see fewer intricate green shapes or graceful contours on them.

Despite the restrictions that make it easier to just bound a circular green, some modern architects will go to the trouble of creating "wings" for "final round" hole locations. Golfers generally interpret these protrusions as unfair ploys to prevent birdies. However, some architects use them to incentivize smart planning and sound execution from the tee by rewarding those who play to a certain spot. In other cases, these strange quadrants are unabashed "sucker" pins to be avoided at all costs. If playing a course where the putting surface boundaries are bizarrely shaped, aerials will help you spot the no-go, code-red situations.

LOCAL KNOWLEDGE PART I: QUESTIONS TO ASK

In golf course design, the obvious thing is always invariably the wrong thing. When we condemn the obvious, it is necessary to remember that no course is really a great course, unless it requires knowing, either on the part of the player or his caddie.

TOM SIMPSON

Augusta National's 12th green is set at an angle that looks slight from the tee.
(Geoff Shackelford)

No other playing fields offer more discoverable quirks and biases than golf courses. Plenty of the nuances capable of messing with your game turn out to be accidental. Some are induced over time by Mother Nature's harsh effects or by random course-maintenance practices, such as mowing patterns or topdressing. If you attribute such little surprise touches to ingenious design layering, architects gladly take credit for all of them.

Often, the local knowledge necessary to overcome obstacles can be surprisingly prosaic. Thanks to your newly heightened awareness of course design and maintenance, you'll now be able to better spot such obstacles or oddities without relying on the experience of those who know every inch of the course.

Yet seeking out knowledge in the right way can pay off. Certain local knowledge mysteries are best solved by making simple inquiries. There is an

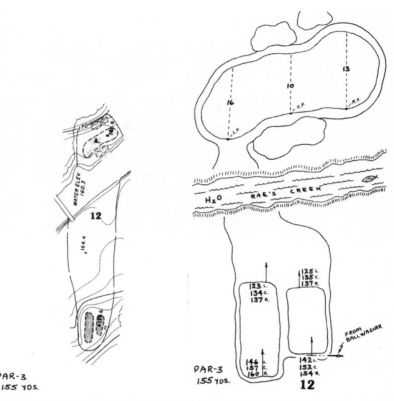

PAR-3
155 YDS.

PAR-3
155 YDS.

12

As an old yardage book shows, there is a 14-yard difference between the yardage to reach the green's left front compared to the right front. (George Lucas)

understandable intimidation factor behind asking a head pro or superintendent a seemingly basic question. Less experienced or skilled modest golfers might even feel it's wrong seeking out course secrets, for example, on the eve of the big tournament.

However, under the Rules of Golf you're free to ask away so long as

The 11th hole, The Old Course at St Andrews is the most famous "exposed" green in golf but does not necessarily appear so at first glance. The Eden estuary behind and slight elevation often makes it putt much faster than the rest. (Geoff Shackelford)

long such inquiries are not made during the round. Most golf pros are happy to answer these questions. Golfers only get into trouble when a question implies that a superintendent or professional is bad at what they do. So preface any inquiries by making clear how you are only interested in solving golf architecture whodunits, lowering your score, and beating opponents who say rude stuff about the pro-shop operation or state of the greens.

Here are some of the more revealing questions to ask industry professionals who likely know the course better than you ever will.

Does the property have a general tilt and how does this impact the break of putts? A remarkable number of courses feature an imperceptible slope. It seems absurd that these gravitational pulls could affect a ten-foot par putt. They do. Layouts near large natural bodies of water, as a rule, slope toward the wet stuff (though you won't know until you ask). The most famous is in greater Palm Springs where everything breaks toward Indio. It's bizarre until you read a putt going one way and Indio pulls it back in! And any design in a location where water once flowed (or still does) is likely to have a stronger incline than you can perceive. The changes in grade will also have profound effects on your yardages and may not be detected by even the best rangefinder.

Are greens at higher elevations firmer? Essentially, a rhetorical question to your superintendent. But this is a great way to guide local experts into sharing insights about how various greens react to shots. Most maintenance crews now do moisture readings and have data to tell the crew which are the driest, and therefore the firmest. The crews may treat some greens differently in the name of reaching greater consistency. But common sense says the putting surfaces sitting higher up are more exposed to wind, drain better and will not hold shots as well as others.

Which greens drain best and worst? This is a more targeted firmness question. If you do ask a superintendent or pro about greens drainage, the responses will tell you where shots are more likely to hold when the green is softer. If you get no advice on the condition of the greens, you can usually find the answer by yourself with an under-foot test. In any case, keep in mind that even with a consistent substructure, no two greens act the same. Nor should they. So getting any information about their condition can be very helpful.

Which hole do they most enjoy watching golfers play? Asked casually with an inquisitive tone, you are likely to elicit a response such as: "No one ever carries over the bunker when they play this hole in the afternoon, and I don't know why they try." But we're getting into an area where the veteran industry professional might become suspicious. Is this person with so many questions trying to get me to admit how I enjoy watching our boneheaded golfers drive into the creek on number 5, when they should just lay-up to take water out of play? Just make clear you're trying to lower your scores, and you should be fine.

Are there any recent courses changes I should know about? Projects to fix design or maintenance issues often go unnoticed by golfers. Asking this will offer a heads-up on how a hole might be playing differently due to changes. Or it could open up other design interest discussion. Just resist the urge to offer your armchair-architect ideas unless asked.

LOCAL KNOWLEDGE PART II: WHAT TO EYEBALL

Every good golf course should have some touches of subtlety that prevents the golfer doing a low score without much previous practice.
ALISTER MACKENZIE

The art of discovering design features brings about the same satisfaction that a hiker might experience when discovering a new view previously unnoticed on a favorite trail. Or when a fly fisherman fishes his favorite pool and notices an undercut in a bank he hadn't seen before—and the delight in knowing it's a classic holding spot for bigger trout. He'll make a mental note, and will never see that pool in the same way again.

Whether it's a slope that feeds a ball into a far-right pin placement, or how superior the angle is into a green from the left side of a fairway, you will file these observations for future rounds. There should be great joy in noticing stuff oblivious to others. Your increased design exploration and heightened awareness will make you a better golfer. Up to a point.

Doodling in notebooks or shaping holes in beach sand? Good news, you have not crossed over. But buying materials to build models of your home course late into the night? Trouble. Big time. That's what pro golfer

Bert Yancey reportedly did with Augusta National in his obsessive quest to absorb every design detail possible. It did not end well.

If you start shaping design features into your mashed potatoes à la Richard Dreyfuss in *Close Encounters of the Third Kind*, you've crossed the line. But I'm confident we can keep local knowledge efforts from taking you down dark paths. Here are some things to scout in the name of self-serving game improvement.

Can I get a visual on where tricky pins are placed? Most courses provide hole location sheets, in the dire hope they'll speed up play. Plenty of golfers own rangefinders. And, unless you've been in a coma for thirty years, then you're aware of ways golfers can grab a yardage via GPS on carts or smart watches. Having the precise number to the hole is certainly beneficial, when the flagstick looks like it could be anywhere on a green.

But even when the target is slightly obscured? Depending on a course routing, note the places where you can get some extra assurance by observing where the hole is located as you walk (or drive) by, including on the entrance road in. Architects have been known to point this out after golfers gripe about an obstructed view into the 7th green.

"You know you walked past the 7th on your way to the 3rd tee, so I won't be crying for you, Argentina." Or words to that effect.

Look long enough and you can spot a sucker pin. As noted earlier, architects will often create wings, tiers, angled areas and other spots only fools attack. Or they will slip in these features or angle the green placement in subtle ways that lure you in. So while the slowpoke in your group is lining up the fourth putt, use this time to make a mental note of flagstick locations where, playing just 20-or-so feet away will leave a simple two-putt. You can also bet the pro and superintendent have identified these final-round pins and may be reluctant to share should you ask. Don't take it personally.

Golfers face a blind second shot into Cruden Bay's 14th with only a small pole as a guide to where the green sits. But below is the view of that day's hole location available when teeing off at the 9th hole. (Geoff Shackelford)

The flag is moving on the 11th at Augusta National while the 12th is laying down. Golfers should always take into account trees and their density in accounting for wind. (Geoff Shackelford)

Which green has the fewest ball mark issues? This suggests either a large green spreading out the traffic or one where golfers tend to under-club approaches. This might also speak to a much firmer putting surface than that of others. And since most golfers fix a ball mark incorrectly (if at all), leaving behind a dead spot, ball-mark damage is pretty easy to spot.

Embrace optical illusions. Golf architects have long endured whining about blind, semi-blind, or totally-barely obstructed views. As Max Behr once wrote, "blindness is a subject that one can go blind arguing about." The modern pro is partly to blame for this obsession with visibility. When they wheel out "everything is right in front of you," it's often just code for "no trickery." With just a little homework, visual obstructions are only blind once. That's why it can be frustrating for architects to hear golfers get hung up on optical illusions instead of embracing the puzzle, applying their big brains, and using these quirks to their advantage.

Accounting for wind. The best players don't even agree on how to play Augusta National's 12th after all these years of swirling gusts and borderline supernatural occurrences. Some say wait until the flags on 11 and 12 are blowing in the same direction. Others say expect the wind as soon as both flags lie down. Others insist you should only tee off on 12 when one flag is blowing, and the other is not. It's called Amen Corner for a reason.

Trees, or a lack of them will play a huge part in how you play a hole when it's windy. Elevated and exposed greens are more susceptible to wind wreaking havoc than a surface set low and surrounded by trees. Or even one set hit high and surrounded by trees. This all seems wildly obvious, but I've seen even the best players in the world fail to account for wind this way.

Also, take note of recent tree trimmings. They're likely to create less of the wind tunnel effect experienced between high rise buildings when air has no place to go. Therefore, wind might be less of a factor.

The point is, using your heightened senses can calculate these local wind-related dilemmas. Embrace the ability to solve these intricacies or file mistakes for next time instead of whining about unfair breaks. It's not easy. But you'll play better.

Green reading. By now, you've realized how often putts are impacted by environmental factors and architectural influences outside of the mown putting surface. Figuring out how shots react or putts break is a skill learned over time. While I'm not suggesting you hire a survey team and spend a minute on each putt while running through a checklist, perhaps your green-reading fits are a result of not accounting for certain factors. Take a second look at how potential externalities can cause putts to do gnarly, unpredictable things. And always avoid blaming the architect or superintendent. They are not the ones making your putter go dead inside, twirl in a figure eight, and then jab-slice at the ball. And apologies for the crude imagery so late in these proceedings.

Remember that rangefinders have their limits. I understand the perks of quickly getting a number to the hole. With a Slope mode turned on, distance-measuring devices even account for changes in elevation. But there is a reason you rarely see elite golfers use them in competition, even when permitted: Yardages to the hole are not as handy as the number to carry a design feature or reach a certain spot on a green.

Here is some key advice after seeing many different courses: Very rarely is the middle of the green a bad place on any golf course—unless it's the Old Course and you're dead center on the 85-yard-deep, 5th green putting to a front or back hole location. So profound is this advice, that I will repeat it: The middle of the green is rarely a bad place to be. If improving your scores is a priority, don't get cute. Middle. Of. The. Green.

Having a yardage to the flagstick can be reassuring and assuage doubts when your view is obstructed. Or when your tee shot found the next fairway over. Just use these pricey contraptions with caution.

If you really want to gain some self-esteem and are just playing for the exercise, try going the Luke Skywalker route and shut down the technology. Use the Force. Fire the golf equivalent of proton torpedo into the Death Star. You'll be amazed at your sense of distance.

A FINAL WORD

Unless you are playing a tournament and need all the intel you can get, embrace the discoverability of golf architecture. Discard some of the pressures the sport induces and trust that informational questions will get answered by time and keen observation. Ownership of this mysterious skill will give you quiet confidence in a sport that can be brutal, humiliating and wildly quittable. The ease in blaming the golf architect or superintendent can be irresistible. Sometimes you won't be wrong for doing so. But, after making it this far, you are a sensible architecture connoisseur who will know when to hold 'em, when to fold 'em, and one who knows a good course after asking three easy questions.

Fairways and greens, far and sure, and happy course hunting,
Geoff Shackelford
October 2022

APPENDIX—LISTS AND RESOURCES

"List, List, O list!"

WILLIAM SHAKESPEARE

After laying out a "system" to accentuate the attributes of far more than the usual hundred or so courses typically recognized, I am obligated to highlight the ultimate places exuding fun, playability, memorability and a certain kind of scale. I present these in the spirit of promoting continued discussion around the world's most fascinating and interactive art form. I do this even as there is little to be gained in the way of upward social, political or financial mobility.

GEOFF'S ULTIMATE, FIRST-TEAM ALL-WORLD R-E-Ds

The places checking off all the boxes. These could also double as my answer to the bucket list course question.

North Berwick West Links. (Geoff Shackelford)

Cruden Bay (Scotland)	The National Golf Links of
Cypress Point (CA)	America (NY)
Old Course at St. Andrews	Prestwick (Scotland)
(Scotland)	Royal Dornoch (Scotland)
North Berwick West Links	Shoreacres (IL)
(Scotland)	Somerset Hills (NJ)
	Valley Club of Montecito (CA)

CERTIFIED, UNDENIABLE R-E-Ds

Places full of memorability, walkability, endless intrigue and a scale my dog would enjoy.

Morfontaine Golf Club. (Geoff Shackelford)

Austin Golf Club (TX)	Essex County Club (MA)
Baltimore CC (East) (MD)	Fenway GC (NY)
Barnbougle Dunes (both courses) (Australia)	Fishers Island (NY)
	Formby (England)
Bel-Air CC (CA)	Formby Ladies (England)
Brora (Scotland)	Fraserburgh (Scotland)
Charlotte CC (NC)	Garden City (NY)
Chicago GC (IL)	Gullane No. 1–3 (Scotland)
The Creek (NY)	Inverness Club GC (OH)
Elie (Scotland)	Kilspindie (Scotland)

Kingston Heath (Australia)	Plainfield CC (NJ)
Lahinch (Ireland)	Riviera (CA)
Los Angeles CC (North) (CA)	Royal Cinque Ports (England)
Meadow Club (CA)	Royal Melbourne (East/West)
Morfontaine (France)	(Australia)
Myopia Hunt Club (MA)	Rustic Canyon (CA)
Newport (RI)	Seminole GC (FL)
Old Moray GC (Scotland)	Victoria GC (Australia)
Olympic Golf Course, Rio (Brazil)	Westhampton (NY)
Palmetto GC (SC)	Wilshire CC (CA)
Pasatiempo (CA)	Winged Foot East (NY)
Pebble Beach (CA)	Victoria GC (Australia)

R-E-Ds WITH A CAVEAT

I'm just not man enough to handle these on a daily basis, but I'll gladly accept a round to double check what are otherwise fantastic places.

Augusta National (GA)	Muirfield (Scotland)
Bethpage Black (NY)	Royal County Down (Northern
California GC (CA)	Ireland)
Carnoustie (Scotland)	Royal Portrush (Northern Ireland)
Castle Stuart (Scotland)	Royal Liverpool (England)
Cherry Hills (CO)	San Francisco GC (CA)
The Country Club (MA)	Sand Hills (NE)
Crystal Downs (MI)	Shinnecock Hills (NY)
Friars Head (NY)	Southern Hills (OK)
Olympic Club (Lake)	Streamsong (Red) (FL)
Pinehurst No. 2 (NC)	TPC Sawgrass (FL)
Pine Valley (NJ)	Turnberry (Ailsa) (Scotland)
Merion East (PA)	Winged Foot (West)

SOME LESS FAMOUS OR OFFBEAT R-E-Ds

Just because you might not have heard of these doesn't mean they are not worth studying.

Pacific Grove Golf Links. (Geoff Shackelford)

Aiken GC (SC)

Anstruther (Scotland)

Bethpage State Park-Red (NY)

Bruntsfield Links (Scotland)

Caledonia (SC)

Common Ground GC (CO)

Coronado GC (CA)

Crail (Scotland)

Delaware Springs (TX)

Detroit GC (South) (MI)

East Links North Berwick (Scotland)

George Wright (MA)

Gleneagles (CA)

Goat Hill Park (CA)

Goose Creek (CA)

Golspie (Scotland)

Huntington CC (NY)

Hyde Park GC (FL)

Leven (Scotland)

Lundin (Scotland)

Los Angeles CC – South (CA)
Lions Municipal (TX)
Memorial Park (TX)
Mid-Pines (NC)
Musselburgh (Scotland)
New Course at St Andrews
   (Scotland)
Pacific Grove (CA)
Palatka (FL)
Panmure (Scotland)
Portmarnock (Ireland)

Pine Hills (WI)
Ponte Vedra Inn (FL)
Rancho Park (CA)
Reynolds Park (NC)
Soule Park (CA)
Southern Pines (NC)
St. George's (NY)
Talking Stick (North) (AZ)
Trinity Forest (TX)
U. Of Michigan (MI)
Wild Horse (NE)

REDs I KNOW ARE R-E-Ds BUT STILL MUST CONFIRM

Some day, some day.

Bandon Trails (OR)
Blue Mound (WI)
Cabot Cliffs (Canada)
Camargo (OH)
Cape Arundel (ME)
Casa de Campo (Dominican
   Republic)
Chechessee (SC)
CC of Charleston (SC)
Cleeve Hill (England)
Gamble Sands (WA)
Lawnsonia Links (WI)
Machrihanish (Scotland)
Mid-Ocean (Bermuda)

Mountain Lake (FL)
Ohoopee Match Club (SC)
Old Town (NC)
Pacific Dunes (OR)
Pennard (Wales)
Royal Porthcawl (England)
Royal North Devon (England)
Royal West Norfolk (England)
Rye (England)
Seminole (FL)
St George's Hill (England)
Sunningdale (Old and New)
   (England)
Swinley Forest (England)

A SELECTION OF NON-EIGHTEEN-HOLE R-E-Ds

More places I'd most love to walk a dog and play fun golf.

Kingarrock—A Home for Hickory. (Geoff Shackelford)

Armand Hammer (CA)	Northwood (CA)
Butler Park (TX)	Peter Hay at Pebble Beach (CA)
Kingarrock (Scotland)	The Cradle at Pinehurst (NC)
The Ladies Putting Club	The Horse Course, Prairie Club
(Himalayas/St Andrews)	(NE)
(Scotland)	Trump Turnberry Resort Arran
Marion (MA)	Course (Scotland)
Morfontaine (Vallière)	Wawona (CA)
	Winter Park (FL)

SHOULD BE R-E-Ds

These gems have been run down too long and would benefit from a refresh.

Cobbs Creek (PA)	Mark Twain (NY)
Eastmoreland (OR)	Montauk Downs (NY)
East Potomac (MD)	Rackham Park (MI)
Francis Byrne (NJ)	Rock Creek (MD)
Griffith Park (Wilson and Harding)	Santa Anita (CA)
(CA)	Sharp Park (NY)
Kebo Valley (ME)	Timber Point (NY)
Langston (MD)	

TEN ULTIMATE Rs FOR REMEMBER

The courses I can recall with ease.

Augusta National (GA)	North Berwick West Links
Cruden Bay (Scotland)	(Scotland)
Cypress Point (CA)	Pebble Beach (CA)
Los Angeles CC North (CA)	Pine Valley (NJ)
National Golf Links (NY)	Sand Hills (NE)
	Shinnecock Hills (NY)

TEN ULTIMATE Es FOR EVERY DAY

The places I absolutely know I'd be content playing daily.

Cypress Point (CA)	North Berwick West Links
Formby Ladies (England)	(Scotland)
Garden City (NY)	Royal Dornoch (Scotland)
Old Course at St. Andrews	Shoreacres (IL)
(Scotland)	Valley Club of Montecito (CA)
Morfontaine (Vallière)	Westhampton (NY)

ULTIMATE Ds FOR DOG FRIENDLINESS

The ultimate places I know a dog would love to walk while I play golf.

Cruden Bay (Scotland)	Morfontaine (either course)
Cypress Point (CA)	(France)
Formby Ladies (England)	North Berwick West Links
Gullane GC (Scotland)	(Scotland)
Old Course at St. Andrews	Royal Dornoch (Scotland)
(Scotland)	Shoreacres (IL)
	Valley Club of Montecito (CA)

DOG-FRIENDLY COURSES OF NOTE

Places in the game well known for welcoming pooches.

Agate Beach GC, Newport (OR)	Indian Valley GC, Novato (CA)
Belgrade Lakes Golf Course, Belgrade Lakes (ME)	Lions Muni, Austin (TX)
Berkshire GC, Ascot, England	Murrayshall Country House Hotel and Golf Club, Perth, Scotland
Butler Park Pitch-and-Putt, Austin (TX)	Peninsula Golf Course, Long Beach (WA)
Chalet View GC, Portola (CA)	Royal West Norfolk, Brancaster, England
Delaware Springs GC, Delaware Springs (TX)	San Geronimo GC (RIP), Marin (CA)
Discovery Bay GC, Port Townsend (WA)	Schoolhouse Nine Golf Course, Charlottesville (VA)
Goat Hill Park GC, Oceanside (CA)	Seaside GC (OR)
Emerald Isle Golf Course, Oceanside (CA)	Skamania Lodge GC, Stevenson (WA)
Goodwood Estate Golf Courses, Goodwood, England	True Blue GC, Pawley's Island (SC)
Huntercombe GC, Nuffield, England	

SOURCES FOR CONTINUING YOUR STUDIES—BOOKS

A Feel for the Game, Ben Crenshaw

A Round of Golf Courses, Patric Dickinson

Golf Course Architecture, H.S. Colt and C.H. Alison

The Golf Courses of the British Isles, Bernard Darwin

The Anatomy of a Golf Course, Tom Doak

The Confidential Guide to Golf Courses, Tom Doak, et al.

Bury Me in a Pot Bunker, Pete Dye

The Links, Robert Hunter

Rough Meditations, Bradley S. Klein

Scotland's Gift–Golf, C.B. Macdonald

Golf Architecture, Alister MacKenzie

The Spirit of St. Andrews, Alister MacKenzie

The Making of the Masters, David Owen

The World Atlas of Golf, Price, Ward-Thomas, Wind, et al.

Golf Has Never Failed Me, Donald Ross

Grounds for Golf, Geoff Shackelford

Masters of the Links, Geoff Shackelford

Golf Architecture in America, George C. Thomas Jr.

The Course Beautiful, A.W. Tillinghast

Reminiscences of the Links, A.W. Tillinghast

The Architectural Side of Golf, Wethered and Simpson

Missing Links, Daniel Wexler

SOURCES FOR CONTINUING YOUR STUDIES—WEBSITES

Cookie Jar (cookiejargolf.com)

Evalu18 (evalu18.com)

Fried Egg (thefriedegg.com)

Golf Club Atlas (golfclubatlas.com)

Golf Course Architecture journal (golfcoursearchitecture.net)

Golf Heritage Society (golfheritage.org)

Links (linksmagazine.com)

UK Golf Guy (UKGolfGuy.com)

BIBLIOGRAPHY

Books full of wisdom that influenced this one.

Browning, Robert. *A History of Golf: The Royal and Ancient Game*. London: J.M. Dent & Sons, 1955.

Concannon, Dale. *Golf: The Early Days: Royal and Ancient Game from Its Origins to 1939*. New York: Salamander Books, 1995.

Cundell, John. *Rules of the Thistle Golf Club*. Edinburgh: James Ballantyne and Co., 1824.

Davies, Peter. *The Historical Dictionary of Golfing Terms: From 1500 to the Present*. London: Robson Books, 1993.

Dickinson, Patric. *A Round of Golf Courses*. London: Evans Brothers Limited, 1951.

Heath, Chip and Dan. *Made to Stick: Why Some Ideas Survive and Others Die*. New York: Random House, 2007.

Horowitz, Alexandra. *Inside of a Dog: What Dogs See, Smell, And Know*. New York: Scribner, 2009.

Lewis, Peter. *Why Are There 18 Holes?* St Andrews: The Royal and Ancient Golf Club of St Andrews, 2016.

Lowe, John L. F.G. Tait, *A Record*. London: J. Misbegotten and Co., Ltd., 1900.

Macpherson, Scott. *The Evolution of the Old Course*. Christchurch, New Zealand: Hazard Press, 2007.

Steel, Donald and Ryder, Peter. *The Encyclopedia of Golf*. New York: The Viking Press, 1975.

Stevenson, Robert Louis. *Edinburgh: Picturesque Notes*. London: Seeley & Co., 1895.

Van Hengel, Steven J.H. *Early Golf*. Vadu, Liechtenstein, 1985.

ACKNOWLEDGMENTS

Ahearty thank you with perpetual gratitude to the superintendents, professionals, managers, secretaries, starters and club members who have hosted me through the years at their sensational facilities. It's been remarkable to watch the transformation of golf architecture, with so many of our treasures treated and revered with the care they deserve. Thanks to all of those out there fighting to leave courses better than they found them. Also, my deepest gratitude to Chris Sulavik for giving my approach to design connoisseurship a whirl by publishing this book and making so many sound suggestions. To those who heard the pitch, read the text or offered suggestions, I can't thank you enough: Glenn Alexakis, Brett Avery, John Blain, Bob Diforio, Alex Galvan, Andy Johnson, David Jones, Russ Myers, Isabella Piestrzynska, Lynn Shackelford and Tim Zielenbach. To Alister MacKenzie, Franklin Booth for providing renderings long ago that were used to liven up the book and to those who supplied images, I offer gratitude and respect for what you do. And finally to my dear late mom, Diane, much love and gratitude for all of the books you picked up over the years that influenced this one. I know you would have loved seeing Ruggles making it into print. Give him my best!

ABOUT THE AUTHOR

Geoff Shackelford covers major championship golf and course design matters in his Substack newsletter, *The Quadrilateral*. A longtime Golf Channel contributor, his writing has appeared in *Golf*, *Golf Digest*, *Golf World*, *Links* and *Sports Illustrated*. In addition to eleven previous books, his golf course design work includes Rustic Canyon, rated the USA's #1 Best Value by *Golf* magazine. As the author of a biography on architect George Thomas, Geoff worked on the multi-year project to restore Los Angeles Country Club's North Course, host of the 2023 United States Open. A southern California native living in Santa Monica, he played college golf at Pepperdine but could never get his beloved boyhood dog Ruggles to stay still during a golf shot. Geoff can be contacted through his website, geoffshackelford.com.